STECK-VAUGHN

DIRECTIONS

An Adult Reading Skills Series

▼ **Larry D. Hodge**

Program Reviewers

▼ **Jewell B. Jennings**
Adult Education/Literacy Coordinator
Wilson County Schools
Lebanon, Tennessee

▼ **Barbara E. Norton**
Executive Director
Project LEARN of Summit County
Akron, Ohio

▼ **Sylvia K. Johann, Ed. D.**
ESEA—Title I Coordinator
New York State Department of
Correctional Services
Albany, New York

▼ **Lynne Porter**
Curriculum Advisor
Division of Adult & Career Education
Los Angeles Unified School District
Los Angeles, California

STECK-VAUGHN
C O M P A N Y
ELEMENTARY • SECONDARY • ADULT • LIBRARY

D0814335

Acknowledgments

Staff Credits:

Executive Editor: Ellen Lehrburger

Supervising Editor: Carolyn M. Hall

Design Manager: Donna M. Brawley

Cover Design: Donna M. Brawley

Photo Editor: Margie Foster

Photography Credits:

pp. 38 and 40 The Bettmann Archive; pp. 44, 45, 46 AP/Wide World; p. 68 ©Roger Prestiy/Keller and Associates; p. 70 poster ©1985 Workman Publishing Company; p. 110 and 112 ©D. Silver/ H. Armstrong Roberts.

David Omer

Park Street

Cover Photography:

©Superstock (balloons); ©Japack/Westlight (compass)

Electronic Production:

American Composition & Graphics, Inc.

ISBN: 0-8114-6397-4

Contents

To the Learner

Welcome to *Directions*. This series of books has been written with you in mind. We've chosen story topics of interest to you. We've presented reading skills that will help you get more out of what you read.

Reading is an interactive process. This means that as you read, you do more than just receive information. You also think about what you're reading, try to make sense of it, and use what you already know to understand the material. Several features of this series will guide you through this process.

• Previewing and Predicting

Before reading each story, you'll look it over quickly and say what you think it's about. Then, as you read, you can compare your prediction to what you find in the story. If you can apply this skill to other kinds of reading, you'll soon become a better reader.

• Writing

Reading and writing go hand in hand. Reading builds your vocabulary and lets you see many different ways of combining words to make sentences. Each lesson in *Directions* ends with a writing page so you can practice the skills you studied in the lesson.

Journal Writing. Your journal is your personal place to keep things you write. Keeping a journal helps you in two ways. First, it gives you a private place to say what you think or feel. Second, you can see how your writing improves as you study and learn. Date each page and keep your writing in order by date.

• Making Decisions

Directions gives you the chance to decide for yourself how some of the stories end. You can decide which direction the story plot will take and write the ending. Deciding what the characters will do helps you practice problem-solving skills.

We hope that this series will help you chart new directions for yourself, and that you'll use the reading skills you've developed in other areas of your life. After reading the stories, you may wish to share with your teacher or classmates your two favorite stories.

When Yolanda looked for a pet, she found

A Different Kind of Cat

Before You Read

Look at the title and photos. Look over the story on the next two pages. What do you think the story is about? Write your prediction below.

_____

_____

_____

About You

Think about things that you like about people. List some of them below.

Things That I Like About People

_____

_____

_____

When Yolanda was a child, she had a pet gerbil. Now she thought she would visit the animal shelter to look for another kind of pet. As soon as she saw the kittens, she wanted to pick up each one. She thought they were really cute.

"You don't want that one," a man's voice said from over Yolanda's shoulder. "It's not as playful as the one in the corner."

Still holding the kitten, Yolanda turned and looked at the man. "I like this one, thank you," she said coolly. *Who did this guy think he was? It was none of his business which kitten she chose,* Yolanda thought.

"The one you're holding probably won't play a lot," he said. "It will just lie around and sleep most of the time. When you think about it, isn't that what cats do? A cat wakes up only for meals, and the rest of the time it shreds your furniture and sheds hair on your clothes." The man smiled. "Don't get me wrong," he said. "I like cats OK, even though they are pretty worthless most of the time. They are better than coming home to an empty apartment."

I bet he doesn't have a cat at home, Yolanda thought. He seemed nosy, but he was nice otherwise. "How do you know so much about cats?" she asked.

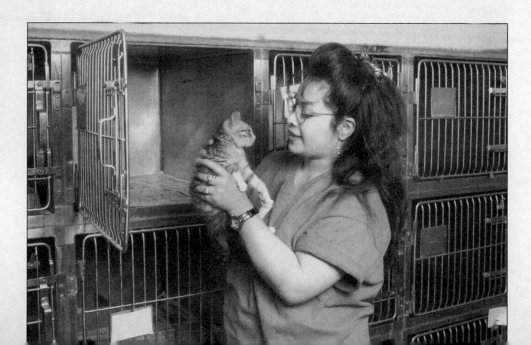

"I work here," he said. "I'm supposed to help people choose a cat or a kitten, if they want one. My name is Tom."

Yolanda laughed. "Tom. Is your last name Cat? You'd have the right name for the job," she said. "I'd like a little more time to decide whether or not I really want a cat. I want to be sure it's the right pet for me. Will you be here tomorrow?"

"Yes, just ask for me if you don't see me," he said.

"I'll see you tomorrow, then," Yolanda said.

"Purr-rr-fect," Tom said.

Yolanda laughed again. As she was leaving, she thought, *I may not have picked out a cat yet, but I think I've met a really nice Tom.*

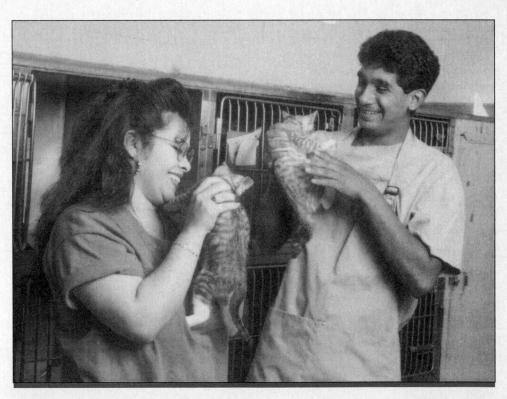

Word Study

A. Consonant Sounds *c, g, ph*

When the letter *c* is before *e*, *i*, or *y*, it can stand for the *s* sound. Read these examples.

ice   city   cent

When the letter *g* is before *e*, *i*, or *y*, it can stand for the *j* sound. Read these examples.

cage   giant   gym

The letters *ph* can stand for the *f* sound. Read these examples.

photo   alphabet

Circle the right word to finish each sentence.

1. Some people cannot (face, fact) the truth about their pets.

2. Those pets can cause trouble any (pack, place).

3. This can happen even if the pet is not as big as an (elephant, alphabet).

4. A friend of mine has a pet (give, gerbil).

5. She never knows if she will find it in the kitchen or in the (cellar, captain).

6. Once she found it in the kitchen nibbling on (clever, cereal).

7. Another friend, Al, had a dog that ate his (perhaps, phone) and anything else it could get.

8. Once Al baked a batch of (ginger, given) cookies.

9. He thought the cookies were safe in the (center, certain) of the table.

10. Later he came home from the (gum, gym) and found an empty plate.

B. Synonyms

Words that have the same, or nearly the same, meaning are called *synonyms*. *Large* and *big* are synonyms, as are *car* and *auto*.

Write a synonym for the underlined word in each sentence. Choose from the words below.

correct	drop	enjoy	final
nap	order	~~pick~~	pretty
stays	tear	want	

_____pick_____ 1. It's not always easy to <u>choose</u> the right pet.

_____pretty_____ 2. Every puppy or kitten is <u>cute</u>.

_____want_____ 3. You may not <u>wish</u> to choose a cat or dog at all.

_____enjoy_____ 4. Either of these pets may try to <u>boss</u> you around.

_____nap?_____ 5. Both will <u>shed</u> fur all over you and your home.

_____final_____ 6. Cleaning up after a pet may be the <u>last</u> thing you want to do.

_____stays_____ 7. If you live in an apartment, your pet may have to <u>rest</u> inside.

_____correct_____ 8. In this case, a dog or cat may not be <u>right</u> for you.

_____enjoy_____ 9. The owners of some buildings do not <u>like</u> the idea of indoor pets.

_____tear_____ 10. They are afraid the animals will <u>shred</u> carpets and drapes.

_____drop_____ 11. Perhaps a bird that <u>remains</u> in a cage would be OK.

Comprehension

A. Main Idea

The *main idea* of a paragraph tells what the whole paragraph is about. All the other sentences in the paragraph give details that tell more about the main idea.

Tips to Find the Main Idea.

1. Read the whole paragraph.

2. Ask yourself: What is the one big idea all the other sentences are about?

3. Reread the first and last sentences of the paragraph. The main idea is usually given first or last.

Read the paragraph and answer the questions.

Tom worked at the animal shelter. He had been there for three years. He fed the animals and cleaned their cages. He also helped people who came to the shelter to find pets. Tom really liked animals, and he was good at his job.

1. Below are three sentences from the paragraph. Which is the main idea? Fill in the circle beside your answer.

   Ⓐ Tom worked at the animal shelter.

   Ⓑ He fed the animals and cleaned their cages.

   Ⓒ He also helped people who came to the shelter to find pets.

2. List some details from the paragraph that tell more about the main idea.

   _____

   _____

   _____

B. Facts and Opinions

A *fact* is something you can prove or see. A fact answers questions such as *who, what, where, when, why, how,* or *how much.* Read this example.

That cat is yellow and white.

An *opinion* is how you feel about something. It can tell how you think or what you believe. Read this example.

I think cats make better pets than dogs.

> **Tips for Facts and Opinions**
> 1. Decide if the sentence tells about something that can be proved or seen. If so, it is a fact.
> 2. Does it have word clues such as *think, believe, feel, seems, probably*? If so, it is an opinion.

Decide if each sentence is a fact or an opinion. Write *F* for fact and *O* for opinion.

_____F_____ 1. Yolanda went to the animal shelter to look for a pet.

_____ 2. Everyone thinks kittens are cute.

_____ 3. Cats seem to be the best pets for people who live in apartments.

_____ 4. The man Yolanda met at the animal shelter was named Tom.

_____ 5. Some cats are black.

_____ 6. Yolanda probably doesn't know enough about cats to take care of one.

_____ 7. I think that some people should not be allowed to have pets.

_____ 8. When Yolanda left the shelter, she had not decided which cat to get.

Writing Skills

A. Journal Writing

A *journal* is a place where you keep your writing. Your journal is for all kinds of writing. You can write your thoughts and feelings about what happens in your life. You may or may not wish to share your journal with anyone. If you share your writing with your teacher, he or she can help you improve your writing. When you look back at your journal later, you'll see that your writing has improved with practice.

Read this journal entry Yolanda wrote after she met Tom at the animal shelter.

Monday, June 13

    I went to the animal shelter to pick out a pet. I really liked the kittens, but I didn't get one today. I want to think some more about having a pet. I did meet a nice guy, though. His name is Tom. I'm going back tomorrow. I hope he'll be there!

B. About You

Tell about something you did or someone you met recently. If you need help writing your ideas, ask your teacher. Keep your writing in your journal.

When you talk to someone, you can tell the difference between
Come-ons and Put-offs

Before You Read

Look at the title and photos. Look over the story on the next two pages. What do you think the story is about? Write your prediction below.

_____

_____

_____

About You

Think about ways you act around people you like and don't like. List some of the ways below.

Ways I Act with People I Like	Ways I Act with People I Don't Like
_____	_____
_____	_____
_____	_____

We use many movements to tell others how we feel without speaking. These movements are called *body language*. If we do not like someone, we may cross our arms or legs while talking to that person. When we think someone is not telling the truth, we may rub our noses. When we want to tell someone "I'm the boss," we try to stand over the person as we talk. When we look into someone's eyes as we talk, we're saying "I'm telling you the truth."

All of us use body language. Most of us do so without really thinking about it. Here are some common examples.

• Penny wants Fred to ask her out on a date. She looks into his eyes. At times she puts her head to one side and puts one hand on her hip. She holds her hands in front of her with the palms toward Fred. She is saying, "I like you. I want to get to know you better."

• Jane wants to get to know Scott better, but only as a friend. She does some of the same things Penny did. However, she looks around the room as she talks. She crosses her arms across her chest. She is saying, "I like you, but let's just be friends."

language (LANG•gwihj) the sounds and movements we use to talk to each other

nervous (NER•vuhs)
not at ease

• Eddie starts tapping his foot when Rose moves near him. Eddie is saying, "You are too close. You are making me nervous."

There's an old saying: "Actions speak louder than words." By knowing how to "read" body language, we can often tell if people really mean what they are saying.

• • • •

Look at the three photos for this story. Which photo do you think shows Penny and Fred? Which photo shows Jane and Scott? Which one shows Eddie and Rose?

A. Vowel Sounds for *y*

The letter *y* is sometimes a consonant, as in *yes*. It can also be a vowel that stands for the *e* or *i* sound. Read these examples.

penny   city
fly   try

Write the word that fits best in each sentence. Choose from the words below.

apply   easy   fancy   happy
hobby   lady   plenty   probably
ready   really   shy   sorry

1. My ___hobby___ is watching the body language of my friends.

2. I like to _____ what I've learned about how people behave.

3. Janet always tries to act like she is a _____ from a rich family.

4. She's sure of herself and not at all _____ around other people.

5. She wears very _____ clothes and lots of jewelry.

6. However, Janet doesn't seem very _____.

7. Sometimes I feel _____ for her.

8. I know she _____ wouldn't like that.

9. My friend Susan has _____ of money.

10. Yet, she _____ doesn't act like it.

11. She likes to laugh and is _____ to be around.

12. She is always _____ to help her friends.

B. Antonyms

Antonyms are words with opposite or nearly opposite meanings. For example, *friend* is the opposite of *enemy*.

Write an antonym for the underlined word in each sentence. Choose from the words below.

common	cross	front	long	louder
~~many~~	Most	nervous	stand	true

_____many_____ 1. We use <u>few</u> movements to tell people how we feel.

_____ 2. If we do not like someone, we may <u>spread</u> our arms while talking to them.

_____ 3. When what we say is <u>false</u>, we look into a person's eyes.

_____ 4. To show people we are the boss, we <u>sit</u> when we talk to them.

_____ 5. <u>Few</u> people use body language without thinking about it.

_____ 6. A woman who likes a man will hold her hands out in <u>back</u> of her.

_____ 7. Standing very near someone can make the person <u>calm</u>.

_____ 8. How we act can send a <u>quieter</u> message than what we say.

_____ 9. When you stare at someone a <u>short</u> time, you may be asking for a fight.

_____ 10. It is <u>rare</u> for a person to use body language.

Comprehension

A. Passage Details

Details tell *who*, *what*, *when*, *where*, *why*, and *how* about the main idea. For example, *Bob* tells *who* in this sentence: *Bob is my friend*.

Look back in the story on pages 15–16 to find the answers to the questions. Fill in the circle beside your answer.

1. To tell others how we feel without using words, what do we use?

   Ⓐ signs

   Ⓑ movements

   Ⓒ songs

2. If you think someone is not telling you the truth, what might you do?

   Ⓐ cross your legs

   Ⓑ look the person in the eye

   Ⓒ rub your nose

3. You stand over people as you talk to them when you want to say,

   Ⓐ "Get away from me."

   Ⓑ "Get ready to fight."

   Ⓒ "I'm the boss."

4. How do people tell you that you are moving too close?

   Ⓐ by crossing their arms

   Ⓑ by tapping their feet

   Ⓒ by looking you in the eye

B. Drawing Conclusions

A *conclusion* is an opinion you form after putting facts together. A conclusion is usually not stated in a story. You have to come up with it yourself by *reading between the lines*, or figuring out what the facts mean when you put them together.

Tips for Drawing Conclusions

1. Read the whole paragraph.

2. Keep the facts in mind. List them.

3. Think about what the facts say to you.

4. Draw a conclusion based on the facts and their meaning for you.

Read this paragraph.

If we do not like someone, we may cross our arms or legs while talking to that person. When we think someone is not telling the truth, we may rub our noses. When we want to tell someone "I am the boss," we try to stand over them as we talk. When we look into someone's eyes as we talk, we are telling them we speak the truth.

I. Find four facts and list them.

Fact 1: _____

Fact 2: _____

Fact 3: _____

Fact 4: _____

2. Which is the best conclusion to draw? Fill in the circle beside your answer.

Ⓐ We use only our hands in body language.

Ⓑ We use body language only once in a while.

Ⓒ We use many parts of our bodies to tell others how we feel.

Writing Skills

A. What Is a Paragraph?

A *paragraph* is a topic sentence plus other sentences that give details about the topic sentence. These details can be more facts about the topic sentence. Or they can be examples of things talked about in the topic sentence. The details should all support the topic sentence. This means they should all tell more about it. Details that do not support the topic sentence do not belong in the paragraph.

Read the paragraph below. Cross out the sentence that does *not* give more details about the topic sentence.

Andy was very good at reading body language. Andy paid special attention to people's eyes and hands as they talked. He could pick out someone who would talk to him by watching the person from across the room. Andy also liked to watch baseball games. He knew how to tell if a person was telling the truth.

Write a paragraph with a topic sentence and detail sentences. Tell how someone you know uses body language. Write the paragraph in your journal.

B. About You

Tell how you can use body language to let people know you are friendly. If you need help writing your ideas, ask your teacher. Keep your writing in your journal.

Parents may wonder how to stop

The TERROR in the Night

Before You Read

Look at the title and photos. Look over the story on the next two pages. What do you think the story is about? Write your prediction below.

_____

_____

_____

About You

Think about things that you remember dreaming about. List some of them below.

Things I Dream About

_____

_____

_____

Nothing wakes parents faster than the sound of their child screaming in the middle of the night. Most children have bad dreams from time to time. Children from about age two to age four cannot tell what is real from what is not. Fears about things they see during the day can turn into nightmares. By doing three things, parents can help their child sleep better.

1. Be careful what television shows children watch. Very young children confuse television with real life. When they see a dog on a show who is run down by a truck, they think the dog is really hurt. Things that do not bother you can still bother a young child. For example, seeing a car crash on TV may not bother you. A child may have bad dreams about being in a crash. Even cartoons seem real to young children. They should not watch cartoons in which the characters get hurt. Finally, don't let a child watch a TV show that might be upsetting just before going to bed. Instead, read a story together.

nightmare
(NEYET•mayr) a scary dream

character
(KAR•ihk•tuhr) someone in a book, movie, or cartoon

Caldecott Medal Winners Since 1980

The Caldecott Medal is an award given each year to the artist of the best picture book for children.

1994	Grandfather's Journey	1986	The Polar Express
1993	Mirette on the High Wire	1985	Saint George and the Dragon
1992	Tuesday	1984	The Glorious Flight: Across
1991	Black and White		the Channel with Louis Bleriot
1990	Lon Po Po	1983	Shadow
1989	Song and Dance Man	1982	Jumanji
1988	Owl Moon	1981	Fables
1987	Hey, Al	1980	Ox-Cart Man

2. Be careful what you say to a child. You might tell a child that if she eats too much she will blow up. Of course, you would be teasing, but the child might believe she really will blow up. Also, it does not help to say things like, "Big boys aren't afraid of the dark."

Adults know there is not a monster hiding in the closet, but a little boy does not. After all, he has seen many monsters on TV and in books. Why shouldn't there be one ready to eat him up when the lights go out? Open the closet door and show the child there is no monster. Let your child know you are near. Leave a night light on.

3. Talk to children about their fears. Help your child learn to tell what is real from what is not. Read stories to your child. Ask the child if a scary monster can really eat children. Explain that some things are only make-believe. Slowly the child will learn that many things are not real. About age four or five, most children learn to tell what is real from what is not. So, they may no longer have bad dreams about monsters hiding under the bed or in the closet.

monster
(MAHN•stuhr) a
huge, dangerous
person or animal

Word Study

A. Vowel Sounds

The *schwa* sound is heard in some words that have more than one syllable. Any of the vowels *a, e, i, o,* and *u* can stand for the schwa sound. The schwa sound always occurs in a syllable that is not stressed. Read these examples.

adult   camel   pencil   lemon   cactus

Write the word that fits best in each sentence. Choose from the words below.

awake   carrots   circus   happen   organ
pilot   sailor   shovel   spiders   tigers

1. When we sleep, the brain does things that it doesn't do when we are ___awake___.

2. We may dream we are huge _____ being eaten by giant rabbits.

3. Or we may dream we can play songs on a piano or _____.

4. One person may dream of being a _____ on a sinking ship.

5. Another may be using a _____ to put dirt in a hole that never fills up.

6. In a scary dream, we may be covered in crawling _____.

7. Some people dream of flying in a plane with no _____.

8. Others dream they train animals for the _____.

9. These people may dream they are being attacked by _____.

10. In dreams, the things that _____ aren't real.

B. Synonyms

Write a synonym for the underlined word in each sentence. Choose from the words below.

accept	dar~~k~~ness	fright
harmed	trouble	

_____darkness_____ 1. Children are often afraid of the underline{night}.

_____ 2. Sometimes fear makes a child wake up at night.

_____ 3. Children think that people really are hurt on TV programs.

_____ 4. A child also will believe whatever an adult says as the truth.

_____ 5. Things an adult says without thinking can really bother a child.

C. Antonyms

The sentences below are not correct. Choose an antonym for each underlined word from the words below. Then rewrite each sentence to make it correct.

parent   believe   fa~~s~~ter

1. The sound of a child's scream can wake a parent slower than anything else.

   The sound of a child's scream can wake a

   parent faster than anything else.

2. It is up to the child to decide which TV shows are OK to watch.

   _____

   _____

3. A child may doubt anything a parent says.

   _____

   _____

Comprehension

A. Main Idea

Underline the sentence that states the main idea of each paragraph.

1. When children see a dog on a show who is run over by a truck, they think the dog is really hurt. They think a car crash on TV is real, and they may have bad dreams about it. If they see a show about a child who loses his mother, they worry about the child and ask if he finds his mother. Very young children confuse television with real life.

2. By doing just three things, parents can help their child sleep better. They can be careful that the child doesn't watch TV shows that could be upsetting. Parents can be careful about what they say to the child, too. They can also talk to the child about anything the child fears. They can explain that many scary things are only make-believe.

B. Facts and Opinions

Decide if each sentence is a fact or an opinion. Write _F_ for fact and _O_ for opinion.

_O_ 1. I think it is scary when kids have bad dreams.

_____ 2. Children can have bad dreams about things that happen during the day.

_____ 3. Children should probably not be allowed to watch any TV at all.

_____ 4. Young children think cartoon characters are real.

_____ 5. I think it is silly for children to believe in monsters.

_____ 6. Most children learn to tell what is real as they get older.

C. Author's Purpose

Authors write for different reasons, or *purposes*. One purpose is to explain something. For example, an author may explain how to help children deal with bad dreams.

Read each paragraph and answer the questions. Fill in the circle beside your answer.

When children see a dog on a show run down by a truck, they think the dog is really hurt. Things that do not bother you can still bother a young child. For example, seeing a car crash on TV may not bother you. A child may have bad dreams about being in a crash.

1. In this paragraph, the author explains

   Ⓐ why parents should be careful what TV shows kids watch.

   Ⓑ why children should not watch TV shows about dogs.

   Ⓒ how seeing a car crash on TV can bother a parent.

When you tell a child that if she eats too much she will blow up, she believes you. Also, it does not help to say things like, "Big boys aren't afraid of the dark." You know there is not a monster hiding in the closet. A little boy does not know. After all, he has seen many monsters on TV or in books. Why shouldn't there be one ready to eat him up when the lights go out?

2. In this paragraph, the author explains

   Ⓐ why children should not eat too much.

   Ⓑ why some children are afraid of monsters.

   Ⓒ why parents should be careful about what they say to children.

Writing Skills

A. Brainstorming and Organizing Ideas

Once you have written a topic sentence, you need to add other sentences that tell more about the topic. These sentences should have ideas and details that explain the topic sentence.

Brainstorming is a good way to come up with ideas and details. When you brainstorm, you think of as many ideas as you can about your topic. You write each idea down as you think of it. Later you can choose which ones to use.

Here are two ways the author brainstormed the topic for this story.

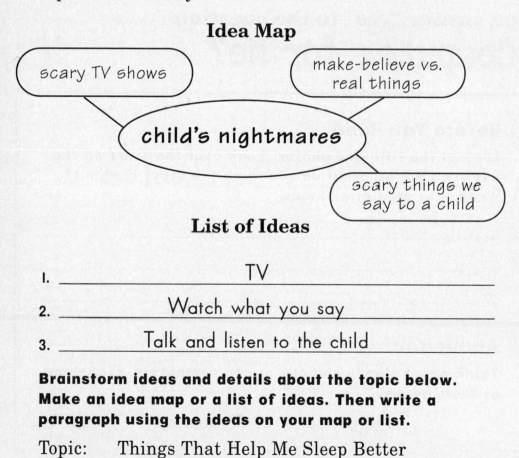

Idea Map

scary TV shows

make-believe vs. real things

child's nightmares

scary things we say to a child

List of Ideas

1. _____ TV _____

2. _____ Watch what you say _____

3. _____ Talk and listen to the child _____

Brainstorm ideas and details about the topic below. Make an idea map or a list of ideas. Then write a paragraph using the ideas on your map or list.

Topic: Things That Help Me Sleep Better

B. About You

Tell about an interesting dream you have had. If you need help writing your ideas, ask your teacher. Keep your writing in your journal.

Would you answer "yes" to the question

Is a Computer for Me?

Before You Read

Look at the title and photos. Look over the story on the next two pages. What do you think the story is about? Write your prediction below.

_____

_____

_____

About You

Think about places you see or use computers. List some of them below.

Places I See or Use Computers

_____

_____

_____

You may think you do not use a computer. However, if your watch shows the time in numbers, you are wearing a computer on your arm. You also use a computer when you play video games or make a phone call.

video
(VIHD•ee•oh)
pictures made for
television

Computers are everywhere. They run car engines. Store clerks use them to ring up prices. Workers in hospitals and workers in steel mills use them on the job every day.

Office computers are used for typing letters and adding numbers. They also store a great many facts in a very small space. People miles apart can share these facts through their computers. This is why computers are taking over the business world.

Computers are also in many homes and schools. People use them to write notes to friends or to do their taxes. Children use them to do homework or to play games. At school, computers help students learn math and reading skills.

But, you still ask, is a computer for me? The answer is yes, someday. Today about half of all workers use computers on the job. This number will grow. More and more, workers will need to know how to use computers to do their jobs.

relax
(ree•LAKS) to rest
or take it easy

Soon computers will change the way we relax, too. Computers will be built into our TV sets. This will let us watch what we want to watch, when we want to watch it. We may even be able to choose a happy or sad ending to a movie.

The thought of having to learn to use a computer scares some people. They should not worry. Computers are becoming easier to use. Today, some computers already work by letting us touch the screen or by listening to what we say. Other computers can read to us. Soon we will be able to just tell a computer what we want it to do. Until then, it's a good idea to get to know how to use computers. They are here to stay.

Word Study

A. Consonant Sounds *wr* and *kn*

Some words begin with two consonant letters, but only one of the letters stands for a sound. The other letter is silent. In words that begin with *wr*, the *w* is silent. In words that begin with *kn*, the *k* is silent. Read these examples.

write   knee

Write the word that fits best in each sentence. Choose from the words below.

knee	**knock**	**know**	**knuckle**	**wrap**
wreck	**wrestle**	**wrists**	**w~~ri~~te**	**wrong**

1. Some people use a computer to __write__ all day long.

2. After a while, these people may feel pain in their _____.

3. The pain means that something is _____.

4. Doctors now _____ that typing on a computer all day can hurt your hands and arms.

5. You can hurt a _____ by bumping your hand on the edge of your computer.

6. Some people _____ with the problem of making the machine do what they want it to do.

7. Sometimes I get so angry I want to give my computer a _____ with a baseball bat.

8. At other times I get down on one _____ and ask it to please let me have my files back.

9. Every time I _____ up a day's work, I wonder if I will ever see the work again.

10. However, my life would be a _____ without my computer.

B. Synonyms

Write a synonym for the underlined word in each sentence. Choose from the words below.

~~auto~~	clocks	cost
motor	shops	work

auto   1. Somewhere in your <u>car</u> is a small computer.

_____   2. The computer helps run the car's <u>engine</u>.

_____   3. Many <u>watches</u> have a computer inside.

_____   4. Today <u>stores</u> use computers for all kinds of jobs.

_____   5. The <u>price</u> of each thing a store sells is kept in the computer.

_____   6. Do you use a computer at your <u>job</u>?

C. Antonyms

The sentences below are not correct. Choose an antonym for each underlined word from the words below. Then rewrite each sentence to make it correct.

~~everywhere~~   grow   rest   small

1. Computers are <u>nowhere</u> you look today.

   Computers are everywhere you look today.

2. The use of computers will <u>shrink</u> as time goes on.

   _____

3. Computers need a <u>large</u> space to store a lot of facts.

   _____

4. After a long, hard day on the job, most people want to go home and <u>work</u>.

   _____

   _____

Comprehension

A. Passage Details

Look back at the story on pages 31–32 to answer the questions. Fill in the circle beside your answer.

1. What do cars have computers for?

   Ⓐ to put air in the tires

   Ⓑ to measure distances

   Ⓒ to run their engines

2. Why do people use office computers?

   Ⓐ to type letters and add numbers

   Ⓑ to learn reading skills

   Ⓒ to choose the ending to a movie

3. Why are computers taking over the business world?

   Ⓐ Computers are cheap.

   Ⓑ They can store many facts.

   Ⓒ They take up little space.

B. Author's Purpose

Read the paragraph and complete the sentence. Fill in the circle beside your answer.

Computers are everywhere. Cars have them to run their engines. Stores use them to ring up prices. Workers in places from hospitals to steel mills use them on the job every day.

In this paragraph, the author explains

   Ⓐ why we need computers.

   Ⓑ some of the places computers are used.

   Ⓒ how people use computers.

   Ⓓ what computers are.

C. Drawing Conclusions

Look back at the story on pages 31–32 to answer the questions. Fill in the circle beside your answer.

1. You can conclude that you

   Ⓐ have never used a computer.

   Ⓑ probably will never use a computer.

   Ⓒ probably already use computers.

2. You can conclude that people in business

   Ⓐ work with many facts and numbers.

   Ⓑ use computers very little.

   Ⓒ do not like to use computers.

3. You can conclude that many years from now

   Ⓐ computers will be used very little.

   Ⓑ people will use computers at work and home.

   Ⓒ computers will be used only for enjoyment.

D. Facts and Opinions

Decide if each sentence is a fact or an opinion. Write *F* for fact and *O* for opinion.

__O__ 1. I think computers have put a lot of people out of work.

_____ 2. Stores use computers to ring up prices.

_____ 3. People who like computers are probably good workers.

_____ 4. Dan feels computers should not be allowed to take over the business world.

_____ 5. Computers can help students learn math and reading skills.

_____ 6. Computers will change the way we watch TV.

Writing Skills

A. Brainstorming Ideas and Details

Brainstorming is thinking of as many ideas as you can and writing them down. Limit your brainstorming to about three minutes at a time to help keep your ideas fresh.

Brainstorm ideas and details about each topic sentence below. Write your ideas as you think of them.

1. I want to learn more about computers.

   how they work

   what kinds there are

   how can they help me

2. People at work use computers in several different ways.

   _____

   _____

   _____

3. There are computers in several machines in my home.

   _____

   _____

   _____

B. About You

Tell about ways you use computers now. If you need help writing your ideas, ask your teacher. Keep your writing in your journal.

Al Capone

Prisons are full of people whose mistake was
Messing Up **Big** Time

Before You Read

Look at the title and photos. Look over the story on the next two pages. What do you think the story is about? Write your prediction below.

_____

_____

_____

About You

Think about people who broke the law that you have heard about. List some of them below.

People Who Broke the Law

_____

_____

_____

Prison inmates often say they are in jail because they "messed up." Most of them mean they messed up by getting caught. Few ever admit their biggest mess-up: Committing a crime in the first place. Here are a few of the famous ones.

Al Capone, Gangster

Why He Should've Gone to Jail. Al Capone was one of the most famous bad guys ever. In the 1930s he broke the law by bringing liquor from Canada to Chicago. He ran a mob that killed anyone who got in its way. He murdered people himself. He stole money. Capone deserved to go to jail because he was an evil man. Yet, that isn't why he finally went to jail.

liquor (LIHK•uhr) drink that contains alcohol

Why He Went to Jail. Capone was not caught running whiskey across the border. Police did not catch him gunning down the boss of another mob. Capone went to jail because he didn't pay his income taxes. Like many people who break the law, Capone messed up. He forgot that everything he did was being watched. He broke the law one too many times.

John La Marca, Kidnapper

Why He Should've Gone to Jail. Kidnapping is a terrible crime. The life of an innocent person is put in danger for money. In 1956 John La Marca kidnapped a baby near New York City. He left a note for the parents telling them where to leave a bag of money. Then he took the baby to a nearby park. He left the baby there to die after he did not find the money. La Marca almost got away with this awful crime. However, there was something he hadn't thought about.

kidnap (KIHD•nap) to hold a person against his or her will

Why He Went to Jail. What did La Marca forget? The note he left was in his own handwriting. He had a very odd way of writing certain letters. Police spent six weeks looking through records at work places, clubs, and schools. They finally found a form that La Marca had filled out telling where he worked and lived. The handwriting on the form matched the note. La Marca was caught and later died for his crime.

George Kelly, Robber

Why He Should've Gone to Jail. George ("Machine Gun") Kelly was a small-time crook. He should have gone to jail for one of the many robberies he pulled. However, he went to jail for a different kind of mistake.

Why He Went to Jail. George married a woman who helped turn him into a killer. Soon after Kathryn Kelly married George in 1929, she bought him a machine gun. She told him to learn how to use it. Kathryn wanted George to be rich and famous. She got him to start his own gang. George and his men robbed and killed. Kathryn often phoned newspapers to brag about things George had done.

George was not making enough money robbing banks to keep Kathryn happy. She had George kidnap a man and demand $200,000 to let him go. After they got the money, Kathryn and George went on a shopping spree. That's when the police arrested them. As George was dragged away, Kathryn yelled, "You rat! You've brought shame to my family."

George Kelly died in prison. Kathryn served her time in prison and was released.

George and Kathryn Kelly on trial.

A. Making Decisions

Do you think people should always be held responsible for crimes they commit? Are there ever times when they should not be held responsible for their crimes?

Brainstorm ideas about each topic sentence and write them below. Your ideas should include examples and other details.

1. A person should always be held responsible for a crime he or she commits.

_____

_____

_____

_____

_____

2. Sometimes a person should not be held responsible for a crime he or she commits.

_____

_____

_____

_____

_____

B. About You

Tell what you think about people who break the law. If you need help writing your ideas, ask your teacher. Keep your writing in your journal.

Review of Lessons 1–5

Word Study

A. Vowel Sounds

Write the word that fits best in each sentence. Choose from the words below.

cactus   camera   engine   lemon   shovel

1. I like a slice of _____ in my iced tea.

2. The thorns of the _____ stuck in his hand.

3. We saw the fire _____ race down the street.

4. My _____ takes good pictures.

5. She used a _____ to dig in the garden.

B. Synonyms

Write a synonym for the underlined word in each sentence. Choose from the words below.

boxes   dirt   shakes   wash

_____ 1. I dropped my sandwich in the mud.

_____ 2. Two large cartons fell off the truck.

_____ 3. Will you help me clean the car?

_____ 4. His hand trembles as he raises it.

C. Antonyms

Write an antonym for each underlined word. Choose from the words below.

hot   right   smooth   speedy

_____ 1. Al rubs his hand over the rough wood.

_____ 2. Do you think this will be a slow trip?

_____ 3. When I touched her hand, it felt icy.

_____ 4. The man gave us the wrong directions.

Comprehension

Read the story and answer the questions.

Most people enjoy ice cream without knowing that it has a very long history. The first ice cream was probably made with snow and fruit juices thousands of years ago.

One of the few Americans who could afford ice cream in 1790 was George Washington, then president of the United States. In 1846 Nancy Johnson invented the hand-cranked ice cream freezer. By 1900 people everywhere were eating the cold treat. Ice cream was no longer a dish only for the rich.

A. Main Idea

Choose the sentence that tells the main idea of the second paragraph. Fill in the circle beside your answer.

① In 1846 Nancy Johnson invented the hand-cranked ice cream freezer.

② By 1900 people everywhere were eating the cold treat.

③ Ice cream was no longer a dish only for the rich.

B. Facts and Opinions

Decide if each sentence is a fact or an opinion. Write F for fact and O for opinion.

_____ 1. Ice cream has a very long history.

_____ 2. The first ice cream probably did not taste very good.

_____ 3. Nancy Johnson invented the hand-cranked ice cream freezer.

_____ 4. I think people today eat too much ice cream.

_____ 5. George Washington was president of the U.S. in 1790.

One word flashed in Diane's mind as furniture flew around the room: **EARTHQUAKE!**

> ### Before You Read
> Look at the title and photos. Look over the story on the next two pages. What do you think the story is about? Write your prediction below.
>
> _____
>
> _____
>
> _____
>
> ### About You
> Think about a time you or someone you know had a narrow escape. Describe the time below.
>
> A Narrow Escape
>
> _____
>
> _____
>
> _____

At 4:30 A.M. on January 17, 1994, people in Los Angeles were sleeping. One minute later over 60 people were dead. Thousands of people became homeless.

At 4:31 A.M., something snapped 9 miles deep in the earth below the city. In the next 30 seconds, the hills near Los Angeles rose over a foot higher. Roads twisted. Bridges fell. Gas and water lines broke as the earth heaved.

heave (heev) to lift with great force

Diane Stillman was asleep when the earth moved. Her room was on the top floor of a building. The building was right above the center of the earthquake. The ground leaped up as much as four feet. Then it crashed back down.

Diane's eyes flew open between the leap and the crash. She saw her dresser flying at her across the room. A second later it pinned Diane to her bed. *Earthquake!* she thought.

earthquake (URTH•kwayk) very hard shaking of the earth

Diane quickly fought her way free. Then she felt herself falling. The first floor had crumpled. The top two floors had crashed into the first floor. Most of the people living on the first floor were killed.

crumple (KRUM•puhl) to crush together

The rumble of the quake had been almost drowned out by the sound of glass breaking and things falling. Then it was quiet, until the screams of trapped people filled the darkness. "It felt like somebody body-slammed me onto my bed and then threw glass on me," said Joanna Killian. She lived in the building, too. "I just stood in my room and screamed."

People dug through the ruins. They helped each other get out of the fallen building. A young man Diane Stillman did not know helped her down a ladder to the ground. Only then did she see how lucky she had been. "Until I was on the outside," she said, "I did not know it had crushed the first floor."

Diane's next thought was of her mother. She ran the three blocks to her mother's home. Her mother was safe. They began the long job of putting their lives back together—and waiting for the next earthquake. They knew it would happen someday.

Word Study

A. Vowel Sounds *ar, er, ir, or, ur*

When a vowel letter is followed by *r*, the *r* changes the sound of the vowel. This vowel sound is not long or short. It is a vowel sound that only happens with the letter *r*. Read these examples.

jar   herd   dirt   corn   fur

Write the word that fits best in each sentence. Choose from the words below.

anger   answer   curb   farms   firm
hurt   stir   work   world   worry

1. Earthquakes can happen anywhere in the
   ___world___.

2. Often people are _____ and property is damaged.

3. There is less damage on _____ than in cities.

4. A person plowing a field might not even stop
   _____ during an earthquake.

5. If you're standing on a _____ in a city during a quake, you may see tall buildings sway.

6. You would be sure to _____ about your safety then.

7. The ground is not as _____ as we would like to think.

8. After a quake, people often show _____ because they had no control over what happened.

9. Such a scare can _____ up feelings of fear that stay with people for a long time.

10. There is also no easy _____ to the question of when an earthquake will happen again.

B. The Suffix -ly

A *suffix* is a word part added to the end of a base word that changes the meaning of the word. The suffix -ly means "how something is done." The suffix -ly is added to words to describe people or things. Read these examples.

quick + **ly** = **quickly**
friend + **ly** = **friendly**

Read the paragraph. Circle the words ending in -ly.

An earthquake strikes so (quickly) it catches people by surprise. That is one reason people are so deeply afraid of earthquakes. One minute people are sleeping quietly. The next minute their world is crashing loudly around them. There are a few things that can help people live safely through earthquakes. For one thing, homes must be strongly built. Also, people should know exactly what to do in an earthquake. Even then, they may barely escape with their lives.

C. The Suffix -ly

Write the word that fits best in each sentence. Choose from the words below.

clearly ~~fully~~ likely
slowly surely

1. Most people are not___fully___ prepared for an earthquake.

2. It is not easy to think _____ when the earth is shaking.

3. During a quake is _____ not the time to be deciding what to do next.

4. You are more _____ to stay alive if you can act without thinking.

5. Move quickly, not _____, to get outside.

48

Comprehension

A. Sequence

Sequence is about time. It means putting things in the order they happen: first, second, and third.

Write *I, 2,* and *3* to show the time order in which things happened in the story.

__2__ Something snapped deep in the earth.

_____ Diane Stillman was asleep.

_____ Diane's dresser pinned her to the bed.

B. Sequence

Look back at the story on pages 45–46 to find the answers to these questions. Fill in the circle beside your answer.

I. Diane Stillman's eyes flew open

   Ⓐ before the earthquake.

   Ⓑ when the ground leaped up.

   Ⓒ before her dresser came at her.

   Ⓓ after she fell.

2. Diane thought of her mother

   Ⓐ before she fought her way free.

   Ⓑ before she felt herself falling.

   Ⓒ after she was outside.

   Ⓓ when she got to her mother's house.

C. Cause and Effect

When you ask, "Why did this happen?" you are looking for a *cause*. When you ask, "What happened as a result?" you are looking for an *effect*. Read this example.

Water lines broke because the earth moved.

Tips for Finding Cause and Effect

1. Look for cause words such as *the reason for*, *because*, *caused by*, *since*, and *why*.

2. Look for effect words such as *so* and *as a result*.

Read the paragraph and answer the questions. Fill in the circle beside your answer.

Earth's surface is made up of many large pieces. Since these large pieces move around, they rub against each other. Sometimes two pieces stick together instead of moving. Earthquakes happen because the two pieces then move suddenly. The shaking in a quake is caused by waves of motion running through the rocks.

1. The *cause* of large pieces of earth rubbing against each other is

    Ⓐ Earth's surface is made up of many large pieces.

    Ⓑ the large pieces move around.

    Ⓒ pieces of earth stick together.

2. The *cause* of earthquakes is

    Ⓐ the sudden movement of pieces that were stuck together.

    Ⓑ waves of motion running through rocks.

    Ⓒ shaking of the earth.

A. Supporting Details

Remember that supporting details should explain more about what the topic sentence says or prove that it is true.

Read the topic sentence and supporting details below. Decide which details support the topic sentence. Mark out the detail sentence that does *not* support the topic sentence.

Many people think that earthquakes happen only in California, but this is not true. Earthquakes can happen anywhere. Many storms happen in the Pacific Ocean. One of the largest earthquakes in North America struck along the Mississippi River. Small earthquakes strike many places in the United States, Canada, and Mexico every year.

B. About You

Write a paragraph that tells about an experience you or someone you know have had with a storm, flood, fire, or accident. If you need help writing your ideas, ask your teacher. Keep your writing in your journal.

Based on what most fast food places serve, their signs should say **GET FAT FAST**

▼ **Before You Read**

Look at the title and photos. Look over the story on the next two pages. What do you think the story is about? Write your prediction below.

_____

_____

_____

▼ **About You**

Think about the fast foods you like best. List some of them below.

Fast Foods I Like Best

_____

_____

_____

Victor was hungry, and the smells in the fast food place made him want to eat RIGHT AWAY! "I'll have a double bacon cheeseburger with special sauce, fries, and a super size soda," he told the clerk.

double (DUHB•uhl) twice as much

"Would you like a fried apple pie?" she asked.

"Sure, why not?" Victor said.

Why not is because in one meal Victor just ordered more fat, calories, and salt than he should eat in two days. After he eats, Victor will let his belt out a notch, pat his stomach, and say, "Boy, I'm stuffed. I don't think I'll ever eat again." But tomorrow Victor will do it all over again.

If Victor keeps eating this way, he'll gain weight. He may get so fat he hurts his health, not to mention the way he feels. Even if he doesn't get fat, he will increase his chance of having a heart attack some day.

Most people eat fast food once in a while. For many people, it is the only way to get a quick, hot lunch on a busy day. The bad news, though, is that about half the calories in fast food come from fat. This fat causes weight gain and heart trouble. Most fast food also has too much salt, another cause of health problems.

calorie (KAL•uh•ree) a measure of the energy in food

Calories and Fat in Some Popular Fast Foods*

Food	Calories	Grams of Fat
Hardee's		
Big Delux Burger	500	30
Fisherman's Filet Sandwich	500	24
McDonald's		
Chicken McNuggets (6)	270	15
French Fries (medium)	320	17
Big Mac	500	26
Pizza Hut		
Cheese Pizza (2 medium slices)	518	20
Pepperoni Pizza (2 medium slices)	500	23
Taco Bell		
Bean Burrito	381	14
Taco Salad	905	61
Taco Supreme	230	15
Wendy's		
Big Classic	580	34
Chicken Sandwich	430	19

*American Heart Association recommends no more than 67 grams of fat for a 2,000-calorie-per-day diet.

It's easy to avoid the bad side of fast food by watching what you order. Here are five ways to eat better while eating fast.

- **Change where you eat.** Choose places that offer low-calorie meals. Have the salad bar or a sandwich on whole-grain bread.

- **Eat roast beef instead of a burger.** If you want beef, lean roast beef has less fat and fewer calories than hamburger meat.

- **Eat your sandwich or burger plain.** Special sauces, dressings, bacon, and cheese have lots of fat and calories. Mustard and ketchup are OK.

- **Don't eat chicken or fish that is breaded and fried.** Most fast foods are fried in fat, which is bad for you. "Extra crispy" chicken is made with even more fat. If you eat chicken, don't eat the skin. It has lots of fat. Chicken nuggets are often made with ground chicken skin. Six nuggets can have as much fat as a cup and a half of ice cream.

- **Eat a baked potato instead of fries.** Of course, this tip works only if you skip the sour cream, cheese, and butter. Top your potato with chopped onions and peppers or hot sauce. Low-fat cottage cheese is also a good topping. Go easy on the salt.

Word Study

A. Vowel Sound *ea*

When the letters *ea* are side by side, they can stand for two different vowel sounds. Sometimes *ea* stands for a short vowel sound. Read these examples.

head   feather

Sometimes *ea* stands for a long vowel sound. Read these examples.

each   meal

Circle the right word to finish each sentence.

1. Most people do not worry about their (heat, health) until something goes wrong.

2. Then they become (eager, eagle) to change their bad habits.

3. It may (reap, appear) that their problems are over.

4. However, they may fail to go (heave, ahead) with their plans to eat better or exercise.

5. It is not (early, easy) to change old habits.

6. You must be (read, ready) to make changes.

7. Then there is a chance you will (increase, cream) how long you live.

8. Often what we need to do is (clean, clear), but how to do it is not.

9. Talking to a doctor can bring (peasant, peace) of mind.

10. You and your doctor should act as a (tear, team) working for your good health.

11. You can start today by exercising and choosing low-fat (meant, meals).

B. The Prefix *dis-*

A *prefix* is a word part added to the beginning of a base word to change the word's meaning. The prefix *dis-* is used often and means *not*, *opposite of*, or *lack of*. Read these examples.

Prefix	Word	New Word	Meaning
dis-	like	dislike	not like
dis-	honest	dishonest	not honest
dis-	comfort	discomfort	lack of comfort
dis-	satisfied	dissatisfied	not satisfied

Write the word that fits best in each sentence. Choose from the words below.

disagree disappear discomfort dishonest
dislike disobey disregard dissatisfied

1. We cannot _____disregard_____ our body's need for food.

2. So, we often wish those extra pounds would _____ by themselves.

3. When we feel _____ because of our weight, it is time to do something.

4. Some people wish they could _____ with that idea.

5. Often people are _____ with themselves for gaining weight.

6. Many of us would be better off if we could learn to _____ sweets.

7. It is best not to be _____ with ourselves when we are trying to lose weight.

8. We have to learn to _____ the little voice inside that says, "You deserve that pie. Eat it!"

Comprehension

A. Author's Purpose

Read each paragraph and complete the sentence.

If Victor keeps eating this way, he will gain weight. He may get so fat he hurts his health, not to mention the way he feels. Even if he does not get fat, he will have a greater chance of having a heart attack some day.

1. In this paragraph, the author explains

_____

Most people eat fast food often. For many, it is the only way to get a quick, hot lunch on a busy workday. The bad news is that about half the calories in fast food come from fat. This fat causes weight gain and heart trouble. Most fast food also has too much salt, another cause of health problems.

2. In this paragraph, the author explains

_____

B. Passage Details

Look back at the story on pages 53–54 to answer the questions. Write your answers in complete sentences.

1. What did Victor order for lunch?

Victor ordered a double bacon cheeseburger with

special sauce, fries, super size soda, and a

fried apple pie.

2. When did Victor want to eat?

_____

3. Why will Victor let his belt out a notch?

_____

C. Cause and Effect

Choose the effect for each cause stated below by looking back at the story on pages 53-54. Fill in the circle beside your answer.

I. The fast food place smelled good,

Ⓐ so Victor ordered a large meal.

Ⓑ so Victor let out his belt a notch.

Ⓒ so Victor went somewhere else to eat.

2. Most people are very busy at work,

Ⓐ so they just don't eat lunch.

Ⓑ so they eat fast food for lunch.

Ⓒ so they gain weight.

3. Chicken nuggets are made with ground skin,

Ⓐ so they taste better.

Ⓑ so most people don't eat them.

Ⓒ so they have lots of fat.

D. Drawing Conclusions

What conclusions can you draw from the story on pages 53-54? Fill in the circle beside your answer.

I. You can conclude that Victor

Ⓐ eats too much fat at every meal.

Ⓑ always eats a burger for lunch.

Ⓒ ordered too much food because he was hungry.

2. You can conclude that people who eat fast food

Ⓐ have no healthy foods from which to choose.

Ⓑ can choose healthy foods if they want to.

Ⓒ do not care about eating right.

Writing Skills

A. Supporting Details

A paragraph has a topic sentence that states the main idea. The other sentences in the paragraph give details that support the topic sentence. There are several kinds of details that can be used to support topic sentences.

Kinds of Details

- *Facts* or *reasons* that prove the main idea
- *Examples* that explain or prove the main idea
- *Things that happened* listed in order

Write a paragraph using the topic sentence below. Choose facts and examples from the story on pages 53–54 to write detail sentences that support the topic sentence.

Topic sentence: I will start eating healthier lunches tomorrow.

_____

_____

_____

_____

_____

_____

_____

_____

B. About You

Write a paragraph that tells what your favorite lunch is. Begin with a topic sentence and give details and examples to support it. If you need help writing your ideas, ask your teacher. Keep your writing in your journal.

Look around and you'll find many ways of
Beating the *LONESOME BLUES*

Before You Read

Look at the title and photos. Look over the story on the next two pages. What do you think the story is about? Write your prediction below.

_____

_____

_____

About You

Think about things you enjoy doing in your free time. List some of them below.

Things I Like to Do

_____

_____

_____

Most people who work love Fridays. Sheila hated Fridays. People at her office talked about what they would do that weekend. Sheila was new in town. She lived alone. The weekend was just a time to sit at home and wish she were out having fun.

One Friday Tim stopped by her desk. "What are you going to do this weekend, Sheila?" he asked.

"The same as usual, nothing," Sheila said with a sigh. "There's nothing to do in this town."

"Maybe you're not looking in the right places," Tim said. "I think of the kinds of things I like to do. Then I look for places to do them."

What a good idea, thought Sheila. As soon as she got home, she made a list of things she liked to do. She liked to be around people, but she liked to spend some time by herself, too. She liked being outdoors, but she didn't like sports. She liked taking care of animals. She liked helping children learn.

Next Sheila tried to think of places she could do the things she liked. She could be around people just about anywhere, so that didn't help. She could stay at home and be alone, so that didn't help, either. And she realized she could be outdoors without doing anything.

This is not helping me, Sheila thought. Then she tried a different way of thinking about it. She tried to think of a place where she could be outdoors *and* work with children and animals. Suddenly the answer came to her. "Of course," she shouted. "The zoo! I could see if the zoo needs someone to help with the animals and to take children around."

Sheila called the zoo. She found out there was a group called Friends of the Zoo. They work at the zoo because they love animals, not because it is their job. The leader invited her to come to the next meeting.

realize
(REE•uh•leyez) to understand

A few weeks later, Tim stopped by Sheila's desk again on Friday afternoon. "I'm going fishing tomorrow. What are your plans for the weekend?" he asked.

"Let's see," Sheila said. "Saturday morning I'm taking a group of kids through the zoo. That afternoon I'm working in the zoo nursery helping to feed the baby animals. And Sunday afternoon the Friends of the Zoo is showing a film on Africa. I love animals, so I want to see it."

"It sounds like you've found a way to keep busy," Tim said.

"I sure have," Sheila said. "Now I can hardly wait for Mondays so I can come back to work and sit down!"

nursery
(NUR•suh•ree)
place where babies
are cared for

Word Study

A. Vowel Sounds *ay, ie, ue*

In some words two vowel letters together stand for one vowel sound. Read these examples.

pay	**Friday**
pie	**tried**
blue	**argue**

Note that in these examples, *ie* stands for the sound of long *i*. In other words, *ie* can stand for the sound of long *e* as in *chief*.

Circle the right word to finish each sentence.

1. One way to keep busy on a (handy, holiday) is to volunteer as a tour leader.

2. Another is to serve on a (rescue, rascal) team.

3. Some people go out and pick up trash along the (hasty, highway).

4. You could bake a (pie, tie) for someone who's sick.

5. Helping others will give your life more (vessel, value).

6. You may also feel that you are (clue, due) for some fun in your life.

7. You could try out to act in a (plant, play).

8. If you do not get the part, your hopes should not (dance, die).

9. People who work behind the stage are the (glue, true) that holds a play together.

10. Get your act together and you can beat the (blouse, blues)!

11. Once you've (tied, tried) doing something, you'll know if you want to do it again.

B. The Suffix *-less*

The suffix *-less* means "without." This suffix is added to the words to describe people or things. Read these examples.

hope + less = hopeless
pain + less = painless

Read the paragraph. Circle the words ending in *-less*.

It is (needless) to feel that weekends are endless. Regardless of who you are, you can find ways to fill up the time. You can give some of your time at a shelter for the homeless. Helping others keeps you from feeling worthless, because you know you are doing good. If you are having sleepless nights because you are friendless, do something! Change a joyless time into a happy time.

Circle the right word to finish each sentence.

1. Having too much time on your hands can make you feel (restless, harmless).

2. Some people get into trouble because they think of (priceless, lawless) things to do.

3. Yet, there are plenty of (harmless, hopeless) ways to keep busy.

4. A (jobless, fearless) person can help with chores around the house.

5. Staying busy helps a person keep from feeling (priceless, hopeless).

6. Taking up a hobby such as jogging can bring (countless, needless) hours of fun.

7. Try not to be (thoughtless, priceless) about other people's feelings.

Comprehension

A. Sequence

Look back at the story on pages 61–62 to answer the questions. Fill in the circle beside your answer.

1. Sheila made a list of things she liked to do

   Ⓐ before she talked to Tim.

   Ⓑ while she talked to Tim.

   Ⓒ after she talked to Tim.

2. Sheila tried to think of places she could do the things she liked

   Ⓐ before she listed things she liked to do.

   Ⓑ when she got back to work on Monday.

   Ⓒ before she thought of the zoo.

3. The Friends of the Zoo showed a film on Africa

   Ⓐ while Sheila took kids through the zoo.

   Ⓑ after Sheila worked in the zoo nursery.

   Ⓒ before Sheila took kids through the zoo.

B. Drawing Conclusions

What conclusions can you draw from the story on pages 61–62? Fill in the circle beside your answer.

1. You can conclude that Tim

   Ⓐ was being too nosy about Sheila's business.

   Ⓑ wanted to help Sheila solve her problem.

2. You can conclude that Sheila

   Ⓐ had not tried very hard to find things to do.

   Ⓑ needed to take a second job to make money.

C. Character Traits

People have character traits. A *character trait* is a way of acting. Character traits are what make people different from each other. Read these examples.

cheerful   honest   mean

Tips to Identify Character Traits

1. Read the story carefully.

2. As you read, look for words or phrases that give clues about how the person acts.

3. Look for actions or thoughts the person repeats over a long period of time.

1. Look back at the story on pages 61–62. Fill in the circle beside each character trait that fits Sheila.

Ⓐ Sheila only liked to be indoors.

Ⓑ Sheila wanted to be with people all the time.

Ⓒ Sheila liked working with children and animals.

Ⓓ Sheila liked to keep busy.

2. Read the paragraph below to identify Beto's character traits. Circle clues.

Beto (whistled) and sang wherever he went. He always had a cheerful "Hello!" for everyone. Whenever there was a hard job to be done, Beto was there to help. On weekends he ran errands for people who could not get out. Beto was never too busy to help someone.

3. Fill in the circle beside each character trait that fits Beto.

Ⓐ Beto was a happy person.

Ⓑ Beto was a lazy person.

Ⓒ Beto did not like people.

Ⓓ Beto was a helpful person.

A. Writing a Paragraph with Supporting Details

Write a paragraph about something you or someone you know does to keep busy and happy.

- Start by brainstorming ideas.

- Then write a topic sentence that gives the main idea.

- Use facts, reasons, examples, or things that have happened as details to support your main idea.

_____

_____

_____

_____

_____

_____

_____

_____

_____

_____

_____

_____

B. About You

Tell about a time when helping someone else helped you forget your own problems. If you need help writing your ideas, ask your teacher. Keep your writing in your journal.

Mary's greeting cards sell

FIFTY MILLION DOLLARS A YEAR

Before You Read

Look at the title and photos. Look over the story on the next two pages. What do you think the story is about? Write your prediction below.

_____

_____

_____

About You

Think about people you know who own a business. List them and the kind of business below.

People Who Own Their Own Business

_____

_____

_____

If you send a lot of greeting cards, the chances are good that one was drawn by Mary Engelbreit. Each December over 7 million of her cards are sold. Her drawing style keeps buyers coming back, not just for cards but also for T-shirts, dolls, wallpaper, calendars, and more.

Sweet is the best word to describe Mary's style. Her bright, cheerful drawings often show cute children. They also have fancy borders. Somewhere in the drawing you can always find her initials, **ME**. The back of each card says, "This illustration is by Mary Engelbreit, who thanks you from the bottom of her heart for buying this card."

Mary, who was born in 1952, started drawing as a child in St. Louis, Missouri. In high school, Mary's art teacher told her she would never make money with her drawings. That bad advice turned out to be wrong. "I decided not to go on to college," Mary said. "I was tired of school. I wanted to get on with working."

In 1970 Mary got a job at a store that sold art supplies. "It was a great education," she said. She got to know many artists. She learned from them that her work was not bad after all. Soon she started selling her greeting-card designs and her career began. In 1983 she started her own business. By 1987 her business was doing so well that she needed help. Her husband quit his job to work with her. Now he runs the business, and Mary does what she does best—she draws.

Mary likes to draw in the afternoons. She spends the mornings making business phone calls. Evenings are spent with her husband and two sons. Sometimes she travels to help sell her products, which bring in $50 million a year. Much of that money is paid to the people who make and sell things with Mary's drawings on them. Yet Mary still makes a great deal of money.

border
(BOHR•duhr) the part around the edge

initial
(ih•NIHSH•uhl) first letter of a name

illustration
(ihl•uh•STRAY•shuhn) a drawing or picture

humble
(HUM•buhl) not
proud

In spite of her success, Mary's sons keep her humble. Once in a store she paid for some things with her credit card. The clerk knew her name and got excited. Mary felt good. When they left the store, one of her sons told her, "You know, Mom, she was just being nice."

If there is one word to describe Mary Engelbreit, *nice* is the word.

Word Study

A. Vowel Sounds *ear, eer, are, air*

Vowel letters followed by *r* stand for a sound that is different from the sound without the *r*. Listen for each vowel sound as you read the words below.

Long Vowels	Vowels with *r*
team	tear
see	seer
came	care
paid	pair

Write the word that fits best in each sentence. Choose from the words below.

~~care~~	career	earn	fair	hair
learn	pair	search	steer	wear

1. Most of us really ___care___ about the work we do.

2. Choosing the right _____ is not easy.

3. We must often _____ for the job that is right for us.

4. Sometimes a friend can help _____ us to the right job.

5. If you like to work with people's _____, you might want to be a barber.

6. If you like to help people choose what clothes to _____, you might work in a clothing store.

7. You could also help someone choose the right _____ of shoes.

8. Be _____ to yourself and keep trying.

9. The secret is to _____ what you enjoy doing and do it well.

10. It's nice to have fun while you _____ a living.

B. The Suffix -y

The suffix -y means "having," "full of," or "like." This suffix is added to words to describe people or things. Read these examples.

luck + y = lucky
fun + y = funny

Read the paragraph. Circle the words ending in -y.

Have you ever gotten a greeting card when you were feeling (gloomy)? Perhaps it came on a rainy day. Knowing someone was thinking of you can make your eyes all teary. Greeting cards do not have to be wordy. Some are corny, or some are funny. But all of them help make an achy heart feel better.

Write the word that fits best in each sentence. Choose from the words below.

flowery ~~funny~~ handy leafy
noisy scary silly sticky

1. Greeting cards can be sweet or ____funny____.

2. Most of us like cards that are so _____ they make us laugh.

3. There's even a _____ card that plays music.

4. If you are _____, you can make your own cards.

5. Dried tree leaves can be pressed between paper to make a _____ card.

6. You might call a card made from flowers pressed between paper a _____ card!

7. Too much glue used to put things on a card can make it _____ and hard to open.

8. A Halloween card might try to be _____ and funny at the same time.

Comprehension

A. Character Traits

Look back at the story on pages 69–70. Fill in the circle for each character trait that fits Mary Englebreit.

① Mary does not value the people who buy her cards.

② Mary is a hard worker.

③ Mary likes to learn new things.

④ Mary is afraid to go new places.

⑤ Mary wants people to like her work.

B. Passage Details

Read the paragraph. Look for details that tell *who*, *what*, *when*, *where*, *why*, and *how*. Then find the answers to the questions. Write your answers in complete sentences.

Mary likes to draw in the afternoons. She spends the mornings making phone calls. Evenings are spent with her husband and two sons. Sometimes she travels to help sell her products, which bring in $50 million a year. Much of that money goes to the people who make and sell goods with her drawings on them, but Mary still makes a great deal of money.

1. When does Mary like to draw?

   Mary likes to draw in the afternoons.

2. Who gets much of the money from the sale of Mary's products?

3. What does Mary do in the mornings?

4. Who does Mary spend evenings with?

C. Sequence

Write 1, 2, 3, and 4 to show the order in which things happened in the story.

_____ Mary started her own business.

_____ Mary got a job at a store that sold art supplies.

___1___ Mary started drawing.

_____ Mary's husband quit his job to help her.

Look back at the story on pages 69–70 to choose the words that best complete each sentence. Fill in the circle beside your answer.

1. Mary decided not to go to college

   Ⓐ after teachers said she would not make money drawing.

   Ⓑ after she got a job at a store that sold art supplies.

   Ⓒ after she got to know many artists.

2. Mary does her drawing

   Ⓐ after her children go to bed.

   Ⓑ before she makes phone calls.

   Ⓒ after she makes phone calls.

D. Facts and Opinions

Decide if each sentence is a fact or an opinion. Write F for fact and O for opinion.

___F___ 1. Millions of Mary's cards are sold each year.

_____ 2. Everyone seems to like Mary's drawing style.

_____ 3. Every card has Mary's initials somewhere on it.

_____ 4. I think Mary is too old to be drawing cute cards.

A. Writing a Paragraph with Supporting Details

Write a paragraph about something you are good at that you could use to make money.

- Start by brainstorming ideas.

- Then write a topic sentence that gives the main idea.

- Use facts, reasons, or examples as details to support your main idea.

_____

_____

_____

_____

_____

_____

_____

_____

_____

_____

_____

_____

B. About You

Write a paragraph with a topic sentence and supporting details. Tell about something you like to do so much you would do it without pay if you had to. If you need help writing your ideas, ask your teacher. Keep your writing in your journal.

Some people have strong feelings in the debate over

GUN CONTROL

Before You Read

Look at the title and photos. Look over the story on the next two pages. What do you think the story is about? Write your prediction below.

_____

_____

_____

About You

What are your feelings about guns? Write how you feel.

My Feelings About Guns

_____

_____

_____

Stu likes to roam the hills hunting deer with his gun. Bud uses a gun to rob stores. Maria has a gun in her car so she can protect herself. Betty sneaks a gun into school to impress her friends. Anna likes to collect old guns. Paul and his gang drive the streets at night and shoot at houses for a thrill. Ron enjoys skeet shooting.

These people have guns for different reasons. Stu, Maria, Anna, and Ron use guns for sport or to keep safe. Bud, Betty, and Paul use guns to make themselves feel important or to harm others.

In the 1990s guns have been used more and more in crimes. Many people want to help stop crime. They think they can do this through gun control: by taking away people's guns or by making it harder to buy a gun. However, other people say, "Guns don't kill people, people do." They say things like, "When guns are outlawed, only outlaws will have guns."

Who should be allowed to own a gun: anyone, or just certain people, or no one at all? That question has troubled people for many years. People who are against gun control feel, "I have a right to own a gun." These people say they have a right to use a gun to keep safe, or

to hunt, or to shoot for fun. People who believe in gun control point out that almost anyone who wants a gun can get one. They say this makes it easy for criminals to get guns. These guns are used against other people in crimes.

Guns are used in many crimes. However, most people who own guns don't use them to harm others. Should people who obey the law give up some of their rights to help protect everyone against crime? People who say "no" point out that many more people are killed by car wrecks than by guns, but we don't outlaw cars. People who say "yes" reply that guns are made for only one thing: to kill.

• • • •

What do you say?

Learn to use a gun safely.

A. Making Decisions

Write a paragraph telling what you think about gun control.

- Brainstorm and list reasons for both sides: for and against gun control.

- Decide whether you are for or against gun control. Then write a topic sentence stating your opinion.

- Write more sentences giving reasons, examples, and details to support your opinion.

_____

_____

_____

_____

_____

_____

_____

_____

_____

_____

_____

_____

_____

B. About You

Tell what you would say to your representative or senator about how to vote on gun control. If you need help writing your ideas, ask your teacher. Keep your writing in your journal.

Review of Lessons 6–10

Word Study

A. Vowel Sounds

Circle the right word to finish each sentence.

1. The (worth, earth) we live on travels around the sun.

2. We each have a birthday once a (year, bear).

3. The ice skater was able to (twirl, thrill) on one foot.

4. The hawk sat on its (perk, perch) in the tree.

5. The fence tore a hole in my (shirt, spurt).

6. I like to sit on the (cord, porch) in my rocking chair.

7. She made me a (stir, firm) offer of ten dollars.

8. The pilot looked at his (chart, charm) to see where the ship was headed.

B. Suffixes

Write the word that fits best in each sentence. Choose from the words below.

extremely	fearless	handy
soundly	spicy	winless

1. The father was _____ when he thought his child was in danger.

2. I was so tired, I slept _____ for ten hours.

3. The food was much too _____ for my taste.

4. Our track team had its first _____ season this year.

5. Cindi is _____ at fixing broken things.

6. Stu was _____ happy that he won the contest.

Comprehension

A. Sequence

Read the paragraph. Then write *1*, *2*, and *3* to show the time order in which things happened.

Sybil went to work early on Friday. She needed to make up for having come in late on Tuesday. The day after that had been a holiday. On Monday she had worked four hours before she took sick leave.

_____ Sybil had a holiday.

_____ Sybil went to work early.

_____ Sybil got to work late.

B. Cause and Effect

Read each sentence. Underline the cause. Circle the effect.

1. We were tired, so we went to bed early.

2. I was late to work because my alarm clock did not go off.

3. Since there are five Fridays next month, I will get five paychecks.

4. The hot sun made us very thirsty.

5. The freeway bridge fell down when the earthquake shook the ground.

6. Thunder made the dog hide under the bed.

7. The ceiling fell in after the water pipe in the attic burst.

8. We moved to this city because I got a job here.

9. The sound of the door creaking sent chills up my spine.

10. The elevator is overloaded, so the door won't close.

*What can you do when someone has hurt you
so badly you think,*

Can I Ever Forgive You?

▼ Before You Read

Look at the title and photos. Look over the story on the next two pages. What do you think the story is about? Write your prediction below.

_____

_____

_____

▼ About You

Think about the ways people hurt each other. List some of the ways below.

Ways People Hurt Each Other

_____

_____

_____

"How could you do this to me?" Kate screamed at Hal. "I trusted you; I believed in you; and now you do this. I'll never forgive you for this. Get out!" She couldn't bear to look at him.

Kate felt better after Hal left, but only for a little while. The anger she felt gnawed at her like a wild animal trying to escape. Finally Kate realized she was ruining her own life. She had to get back to normal, but to do that she had to do something very difficult. She needed to forgive Hal for hurting her.

gnaw (naw) to chew

• • • •

Kate got help in solving her problem and learned what she had to do to forgive Hal. She talked to her friend Barbara many times. Kate told Barbara what had happened and how angry she felt. Barbara listened to everything and said she understood. Barbara also said that somehow Kate had to talk things over with Hal and forgive him.

• • • •

Finally, Kate had a talk with Hal. "You lied to me, Hal," she said. "You broke the promise we made never to lie to each other."

"You're right, Kate," Hal said, "and I'm very sorry I did that, because I know it hurt you a lot."

"Yes, it did," Kate replied, "but that wasn't the only thing. As I looked to the future, I saw that I couldn't trust you anymore. You took away my trust."

Hal said nothing, but he bowed his head sadly and nodded.

Kate's anger came rushing back. "This whole thing was your fault," she yelled. "If you had just told me the truth, I would've been angry, but that would've passed.

When you lied to me, it destroyed my trust in you, and that was the worst blow."

"It was my fault," Hal said. "How can I make it up to you?"

"I don't know," Kate said. "I've done whatever you wanted and put you first, but now I'm going to start putting myself first. I've always wanted to take some art classes, and I'm going to do it. Maybe you can make it up to me by helping with the housework and getting your own supper. And do one more thing: Promise never to lie to me again."

"I won't, Kate. I promise," Hal said.

"OK. I accept your promise," Kate replied. "And I won't bring this up again. Let's put it behind us and get on with our lives."

"Thank you for forgiving me, Kate," Hal said. "I'll make sure nothing like this ever happens again."

Word Study

A. Vowel Sounds *au*, *aw*, *al*, *all*

The letters *au*, *aw*, *al*, and *all* stand for the vowel sound heard in *tall*. Read these examples.

fault   claw   always   tall

Write the word that fits best in sentence. Choose from the words below.

also   awful   awkward   caught
cause   dawn   fault   small
stall   talk   walk

1. It is hard to admit something is our _____fault_____.

2. However, it can be even worse to be _____ in a lie.

3. Often people _____ as long as they can before talking about a problem.

4. This can make life very _____ for both people.

5. It _____ makes the problem worse.

6. It is better to _____ about problems while they are still small.

7. Otherwise, they can _____ more problems between people.

8. A _____ problem may get bigger if you let it go.

9. A good rule is never to let a new day _____ on an old problem.

10. Most people feel _____ as long as they are angry.

11. You should try not to _____ away from a problem.

B. Multiple Meanings

A word can have *multiple meanings*, or more than one meaning. To decide which meaning fits the sentence you are reading, look at the other words in the sentence. Think about how the word is used in the sentence.

Look at four different meanings for *bear*:

a. to carry

b. to put up with

c. a large animal

d. to produce

Write the letter of the meaning that best fits the way *bear* is used in each sentence.

__d__ 1. I hope that tree will bear fruit this year.

_____ 2. I don't know how much longer I can bear this noise.

_____ 3. The bear came into our camp looking for food.

_____ 4. This wall is not strong enough to bear the weight of the roof.

C. Multiple Meanings

Look at three different meanings for blow:

a. to send forth air from the mouth

b. a shock or bad happening

c. to be carried by the wind

Write the letter of the meaning that best fits the way *blow* is used in each sentence.

_____ 1. The loss of a friend can be a hard blow.

_____ 2. I blow on my coffee to cool it before I drink it.

_____ 3. That plant in the window could blow over.

Comprehension

A. Passage Details

Look back at the story on pages 83-84 to find the answers to the questions. Fill in the circle beside your answer.

1. Who did something that hurt the other person?

   Ⓐ Kate hurt Hal.

   🅑 Hal hurt Kate.

   Ⓒ Kate and Hal's son hurt them.

2. What did Hal do that destroyed Kate's trust in him?

   Ⓐ He told her the truth.

   Ⓑ He told her a lie.

   Ⓒ He blamed her for his mistake.

3. How did Kate say she would make their lives different?

   Ⓐ She would keep blaming Hal.

   Ⓑ She would not accept Hal's promise.

   Ⓒ She would put herself first.

B. Main Idea

Underline the sentence that states the main idea of each paragraph.

1. It is usually better to forgive someone who has hurt you. As long as you stay angry, you are hurting yourself. Also, your anger becomes a second problem. So then you have two problems, being hurt and being angry.

2. Kate was angry. She had been hurt, and she could not get over it. She was also upset with herself for feeling this way. She couldn't sleep or do her work. Kate had to forgive Hal to make things right again.

C. Sequence

Look back at the story on pages 83–84 to find the answers to the questions. Fill in the circle beside your answer.

I. At first Kate felt better

   (A) before Hal left.

   (B) after Hal left.

   (C) while she was screaming at Hal.

2. Kate realized she was ruining her own life

   (A) before Hal left.

   (B) after she forgave Hal.

   (C) before she talked to Barbara.

D. Drawing Conclusions

Find three facts and list them below.

Kate's anger came rushing back. "This whole thing was your fault," she yelled. "If you had just told me the truth, I would have been angry, but that would have passed. When you lied to me, it destroyed my trust in you, and I blame you for that."

Fact 1: ___Kate said the whole thing was Hal's fault.___

Fact 2: _____

Fact 3: _____

Which is the best conclusion to draw? Fill in the circle beside your answer.

   ① Kate will never get over being angry at Hal.

   ② Things would have been better if Hal had not lied.

   ③ Hal had not really done anything wrong.

Writing Skills

A. Writing Advice

Kate and Hal went to see a counselor to learn how to treat each other better. Hal took notes about things they learned. Later he made this idea map.

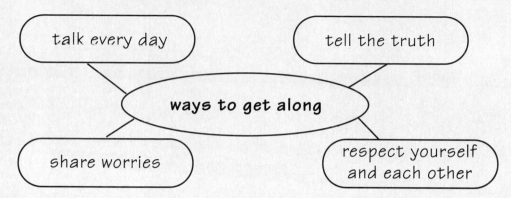

After making the idea map, Hal expanded the ideas into sentences. Then he added details about Kate, himself, and their problem.

Write a paragraph that Hal might have written using his idea map. Start with the topic sentence below.

There are four things Kate and I can do to get along better.

_____

_____

_____

_____

_____

_____

_____

B. About You

Tell about how you and another person solved a problem by talking about it. If you need help writing your ideas, ask your teacher. Keep your writing in your journal.

LESSON 12

The job of being a parent gets even harder
When Two Families Become One

Before You Read

Look at the title and photos. Look over the story on the next two pages. What do you think the story is about? Write your prediction below.

_____

_____

_____

About You

Think about things that often lead to arguments in your family. List some of them below.

Things My Family Argues About

_____

_____

_____

"Dana, please don't set that wet glass on the coffee table," Marge said. "It'll leave a ring."

Dana looked at her stepmother, and her bottom lip began to tremble. "You're so mean to me," she said. "I wish my real mother were here!" She ran from the room crying.

Marge looked at her new husband, Jim, and spread her hands as if to ask, "What did I do to make her so upset?"

Actually, Marge had done the right thing. She wouldn't have let her own children put a wet glass on the table. She shouldn't let her stepdaughter do it, either.

By putting the glass on the table, Dana was testing Marge. Dana was really saying, "If you love me, you won't let me do this." Dana will test Marge many times before she finally behaves better.

Remarried parents who bring children to a new marriage face many such problems. Here is how experts suggest handling some of the most common problems.

Who should make the children behave? Parents must find out what works with their children. Sometimes it is best to let each birth parent make his or her own children behave. Very young children may behave for either parent. However, all children shouldn't be treated exactly alike. Each child should be treated as a different person. Older children can be allowed to stay up later than younger children, for example.

What should children call the stepparent? A child shouldn't be forced to call a new stepparent "Mom" or "Dad." The child still needs to love his or her real parent. One way to handle this is to suggest the child call the stepparent by his or her first name. Some children like to use a nickname like "Daddy Jim."

stepmother (STEHP•muhther) a woman married to one's real father

stepdaughter (STEHP•dawter) the daughter of the person one is married to

stepparent (stehp•PAR•uhnt) a person who has married one's real mother or father

Should the stepparent adopt children from the other marriage? Some people try to prove to the children that they are part of a "real" family by giving the same last name to all the children. Some children don't like this, since it seems to say that their birth parent isn't important. Let children decide for themselves when they're 16 or older.

If the new marriage is good for the parents, it will be good for the children. Children just need time to adjust to having a new parent.

Word Study

A. Silent Consonants *gh*

When the letters *gh* come after a vowel sound, they are silent. Read these examples.

bought   daughter   high   weigh

Write the word that fits best in each sentence. Choose from the words below.

brought	delight	~~fights~~	might
neighbor	right	sigh	though
thought	through	weight	

1. Questions about how to handle stepchildren lead to many family ____fights____.

2. Fights can be avoided by giving the matter some _____.

3. Many parents think they always have to be _____.

4. Very few of us are perfect, _____.

5. Accepting this fact can take a great _____ off a parent's shoulders.

6. Parents can't solve every problem _____ to them.

7. Try as we _____, there are times when we need to ask for advice.

8. Often a next-door _____ can help.

9. Just a friendly talk can help us get _____ the day.

10. When we're calmer, our children are once again the _____ of our lives.

11. With a _____, we wonder what all the fuss was about.

B. Multiple Meanings

Choose the meaning that best fits the way *set* is used in the sentence. Fill in the circle beside your answer.

1. Each night I set the table before dinner.

   Ⓐ to arrange silverware on a table

   Ⓑ to become hard

2. The actor bumped into the set and knocked it over.

   Ⓐ to become hard

   Ⓑ the scenery on a stage

3. The set of dishes was very expensive.

   Ⓐ to decide a time or amount

   Ⓑ a group of people or things

4. We had to smooth the cement before it set.

   Ⓐ to become hard

   Ⓑ to go down

5. Have you set the prices for your garage sale?

   Ⓐ a group of persons or things

   Ⓑ to decide a time or amount

6. She set the computer on her desk.

   Ⓐ to put in a place

   Ⓑ to arrange silverware on a table

7. You can win if you set your mind to it.

   Ⓐ a group of persons or things

   Ⓑ to become determined

8. We watched the sun set over the lake.

   Ⓐ the scenery on a stage

   Ⓑ to go down

Comprehension

A. Passage Details

Look back at the story on pages 91–92 to find the answers to the questions. Fill in the circle beside your answer.

1. What did Marge and Dana argue about?

    Ⓐ the other children

    Ⓑ a wet glass

2. Who ran from the room crying?

    Ⓐ Dana

    Ⓑ Marge

3. When should stepchildren decide whether to be adopted ?

    Ⓐ as soon as possible after their parents marry

    Ⓑ after thcy reach the age of 16

B. Main Idea

Rcad the paragraph. Underline the sentence with the main idea.

1. A child shouldn't be made to call a new stepparent "Mom" or "Dad." The child still needs to love his or her real parent. One way to handle this is to suggest the child call the stepparent by his or her first name. Some children like to use a name like "Daddy Jim."

2. Some people try to prove to the children that they are part of a "real" family by giving the same last name to all the children. Some children don't like this, since it seems to say their birth parent isn't important. Children should decide for themselves when they are 16 or older.

C. Author's Purpose

Look back at the story on pages 91–92. Choose the words that best complete each sentence. Fill in the circle beside your answer.

1. The author's purpose for writing the story was to show

   Ⓐ parents how to handle bad kids.

   Ⓑ that being a parent is hard.

   Ⓒ that stepchildren have a hard time.

   Ⓓ stepparents how to handle common problems.

2. The author's purpose for writing paragraph five on page 91 about making children behave was to show that

   Ⓐ children must be made to behave.

   Ⓑ this is an easy part of parenting.

   Ⓒ one parent must do this job.

   Ⓓ children are different.

D. Drawing Conclusions

What conclusions can you draw from the story on pages 91–92? Fill in the circle beside your answer.

1. You can conclude that Marge and Jim

   Ⓐ got married recently.

   Ⓑ have been married a long time.

   Ⓒ are thinking of getting a divorce.

2. You can conclude that Dana

   Ⓐ is a bad child.

   Ⓑ is trying to make sure Marge loves her.

   Ⓒ is a silly teenager.

Writing Skills

A. Writing Advice

Imagine that you are a single parent who gets remarried. Your new husband or wife also has children.

Brainstorm a list of ideas or advice that would help everyone in the new family get along. Make an idea map of your ideas below.

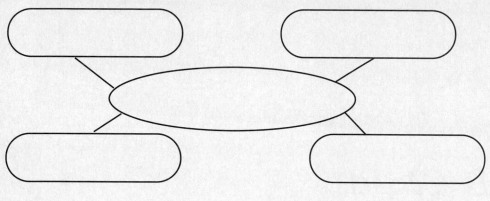

Write a topic sentence for a paragraph based on your ideas.

_____

_____

_____

_____

B. About You

Write a paragraph using the topic sentence you wrote above. Use your idea map to write the other sentences in the paragraph. If you need help writing your ideas, ask your teacher. Keep your writing in your journal.

In This Child

Before You Read

Look at the title and photo. Look over the poem on the next page. What do you think the poem is about? Write your prediction below.

_____

_____

_____

About You

Think about ways your parents or children affect your life. List some ways below.

Ways My Parents or Children Affect My Life

_____

_____

_____

In This Child

In this child so small I see
The little boy that once was me.
His eyes so bright and full of life
Have yet to gaze on bitter strife.

He is a storm that jumps and runs,
Drives toy trucks and shouts in fun.
In this he is, like little boys all,
His dad made over, only small.

We go each day to play and tumble,
To sounds of traffic's honk and rumble.
As we walk home from the park,
He is the light that warms the dark.

As I shape him, so he shapes me.
Though separate branches, we are one tree.
And as I look at him I wonder,
Is he the lightning, or the thunder?

strife (streyef)
fighting or arguing

Word Study

Words in Context

Context means all the words in a sentence or paragraph. You can use context to help you figure out the meaning of a word you don't know. Look at all the other words that are around the new word to decide what that word must mean. Read this example.

The <u>strife</u> between countries sometimes leads to war.

- Could *strife* mean "peace"? (Clue: Look at the clue words *leads to war* in the sentence. *Peace* would not make sense.)

- Could *strife* mean "arguments"? (Clue: *Arguments* would make sense with the clue words *leads to war*.)

> **Tips to Figure Out Words in Context**
>
> I. Read the sentence to the end. Don't stop at the new word.
>
> 2. Think about what meaning makes sense.

Read the sentence. Circle the word or words that have almost the same meaning as the underlined word.

I. Tom's <u>gaze</u> followed Liz around the room.

   sign   (look)   walk

2. We watched the bridge <u>collapse</u> into the water below.

   rise   stand   fall

3. Jay was <u>plagued</u> by many small accidents.

   helped   given   troubled

4. The cabin was so <u>remote</u> that she had to travel many miles to reach it.

   far away   small   large

Comprehension

A. Character Traits

Look back at the poem on page 99 to complete the sentences. Fill in the circle beside the character trait that best fits the little boy.

1. The boy is

   Ⓐ sad.

   Ⓑ lively.

   Ⓒ fearful.

   Ⓓ bad.

2. The boy is

   Ⓐ young.

   Ⓑ tall.

   Ⓒ rude.

   Ⓓ careless.

B. Drawing Conclusions

What conclusions can you draw from the poem on page 99? Fill in the circle beside your answer.

1. You can conclude that the poem was written by

   Ⓐ the little boy.

   ● the little boy's father.

   Ⓒ the little boy's mother.

2. You can conclude that the father

   Ⓐ pays little attention to his son.

   Ⓑ plays with his son every day.

   Ⓒ does not live with his son.

3. You can conclude that the father and son

   Ⓐ are not alike in any way.

   Ⓑ are alike in many ways.

   Ⓒ do not want to be like each other.

C. Figurative Language with Metaphors

A *metaphor* compares two things that are not alike, but it does not use the words *like* or *as*. A metaphor says that one thing <u>is</u> another thing. You may recall that a simile does use *like* or *as* to compare two things. Read these examples.

Simile: The night is like a curtain that falls over the land.

Metaphor: The night is a curtain that falls over the land.

In the examples, the metaphor says that *night* <u>is</u> a *curtain*.

Read the poem. Look for metaphors. Then complete each sentence below. Fill in the circle beside your answer.

> The wind is my sweet bedtime song,
> To sleep it carries me along.
> Yet in the night it is a battle
> Making all the windows rattle.

1. In the first two lines, the wind is called

    Ⓐ a person.

    Ⓑ a bed.

    Ⓒ a song.

2. In the last two lines, the wind is called

    Ⓐ a window.

    Ⓑ a battle.

    Ⓒ a night.

Writing Skills

A. Writing Metaphors

Brainstorm a list of things you would like to describe using metaphors. Write the list below.

1. _____children_____
2. _____
3. _____
4. _____
5. _____
6. _____
7. _____
8. _____
9. _____
10. _____

Write metaphors using the things from your list.

1. _____Children are crickets that jump all around._____
2. _____
3. _____
4. _____
5. _____
6. _____
7. _____
8. _____
9. _____
10. _____

B. About You

Describe yourself using metaphors. If you need help writing your ideas, ask your teacher. Keep your writing in your journal.

LESSON 14

A Friend Is...

▼ Before You Read

Look at the title and photo. Look over the poem on the next page. What do you think the poem is about? Write your prediction below.

_____

_____

_____

▼ About You

Think about things you look for in a friend. List some of them below.

Things I Look for in a Friend

_____

_____

_____

A Friend Is . . .

A friend is a rock that never crumbles,
A cloud that never rains,
A mount that never stumbles,
A bond that still remains.

A friend is a road that never ends,
A river that runs so deep,
A tree that never bends,
A treasure meant to keep.

A friend is a gift myself I give,
A prize I hope to win,
A safe place that I can live,
A guest I welcome in.

A friend is my own perfect self,
A person I'd like to be,
A trophy sitting on a shelf,
A mirror reflecting me.

mount (mownt) a
horse someone
rides

bond (bahnd)
something that ties
two things
together

Word Study

Vowel Sounds *ou*, *ow*

The letters *ou* and *ow* sometimes stand for the vowel sound in *house*. Read these examples.

cloud	out	mountain
allow	down	how

Write the word that fits best in each sentence. Choose from the words below.

blouse	brown	couch	cowboy
doubt	flowers	~~found~~	However
Now	outfits	sound	

1. Tina is lucky to have __found__ Vicki for a friend.

2. _____ Tina can borrow Vicki's clothes for dates.

3. Vicki has a red _____ that really looks good on Tina.

4. Some of Vicki's _____ can surprise Ed, the guy Tina dates.

5. Once Ed was sitting on the _____ when Tina walked in.

6. She was wearing a dress with huge purple

   _____.

7. I think he began to _____ what he saw!

8. He tried to speak but couldn't make a _____.

9. _____, Ed wears some pretty odd clothes himself.

10. Sometimes he wears sneakers and a black

    _____ hat.

11. Other times he wears a green shirt with _____ stripes.

Comprehension

A. Drawing Conclusions

What conclusions can you draw from these lines of the poem? Fill in the circle beside your answer.

> A friend is a rock that never crumbles,
> A cloud that never rains,
> A mount that never stumbles,
> A bond that still remains.

1. You can conclude that a friend

   Ⓐ never falls down.

   Ⓑ is always there.

   Ⓒ comes and goes.

> A friend is my own perfect self,
> A person I'd like to be,
> A trophy sitting on a shelf,
> A mirror reflecting me.

2. You can conclude that a friend is

   Ⓐ something unlucky.

   Ⓑ something you can win.

   Ⓒ something valuable.

B. Facts and Opinions

Decide if each sentence is a fact or an opinion. Write *F* for fact and *O* for opinion.

_O_ 1. Friends are always better people than we are ourselves.

_____ 2. My best friend and I met in high school.

_____ 3. Their friendship will probably not last very long.

_____ 4. Jack and Jim have been friends for 12 years.

C. Figurative Language with Metaphors

Read the lines from the poem. Circle the things a friend is compared to.

1. A friend is a (rock) that never crumbles,

   A (cloud) that never rains,

   A (mount) that never stumbles,

   A (bond) that still remains.

2. A friend is a road that never ends,

   A river that runs so deep,

   A tree that never bends,

   A treasure meant to keep.

3. A friend is a gift myself I give,

   A prize I hope to win,

   A safe place that I can live,

   A guest I welcome in.

D. Figurative Language with Metaphors

Read each metaphor. Circle the two things that are compared.

1. My (car) is a (magic carpet)

   That takes me for a ride.

2. His words were knives

   Slashing my very soul.

3. The snake is a question mark

   Wriggling across the sand.

4. My joy is a balloon

   Rising in the air.

Writing Skills

A. Writing Metaphors

Brainstorm a list of things about people you could describe using metaphors. Write the list below.

1. _____ eyes _____
2. _____
3. _____
4. _____
5. _____
6. _____
7. _____
8. _____
9. _____
10. _____

Write metaphors using things from your list.

1. _____ Mary's eyes are sparkling diamonds. _____
2. _____
3. _____
4. _____
5. _____
6. _____
7. _____
8. _____
9. _____
10. _____

B. About You

Describe someone you know using metaphors. If you need help writing your ideas, ask your teacher. Keep your writing in your journal.

Anyone who has seen performers
"saw a woman in half" has wondered

How Do They Do That?

Before You Read

Look at the title and photos. Look over the story on the next two pages. What do you think the story is about? Write your prediction below.

_____

_____

_____

About You

Think about magic tricks you have seen or heard about. List some of them below.

Magic Tricks I Have Seen or Heard About

_____

_____

_____

Magic tricks please people of all ages. Young children think that a magician really <u>can</u> pull a rabbit out of a hat, make a person float in the air, or saw a woman in half. We know such things cannot be done. However, we still enjoy the tricks and want to know how they work.

Some magicians perform their tricks as a job. They are called professional magicians. You can see them on TV, in theaters, and in comedy clubs. Sometimes they are even hired to bring some fun to business meetings. Other magicians do tricks as a hobby. They often perform for people at parties.

Magic tricks have been around for a long time. The first time a magician pulled a rabbit out of a hat was in France about 175 years ago. The first magician who seemed to saw a woman in half did so in London, England, in 1920. P.T. Selbit put a woman in a long box with her head sticking out of one end of the box. She just drew her knees up under her chin during the sawing. Later magicians used two women for this trick. One woman was in the box. The other woman hid in the thick table top. As the magician spun the table, the woman in the box pulled her feet up. Then the other woman stuck her feet out. This trick let the second woman wiggle her feet after they had been "cut off."

In 1982 Doug Henning, a magician from Canada, tried a new way to do this old trick. He used a pair of fake feet. They were attached to a board inside the box. As the woman's feet were turned so they could not be seen, she pulled them inside the box. Then the woman kicked the board out so the fake feet showed. After the sawing was done, the woman pulled on a string to wiggle the fake feet.

Another magician had the woman lie on a table instead of being inside a box. She wore a stiff dress that kept the shape of her body while she sank into a long

magician (muh•JISH•uhn) person who does magic tricks

professional (proh•FEHSH•uh•nuhl) done as a job

hole in the table top. Then the saw passed over her back and didn't really touch her at all.

To pull a rabbit out of a hat, a magician must have fast hands. The magician uses a rabbit because it is a quiet animal. He puts a live rabbit in a bag hung from the table where people cannot see the bag. Someone looks into a hat to prove it is empty. Then the magician takes the hat in one hand and the bag with the rabbit in the other hand. As he moves the hat around, he swings the bag with the rabbit into the hat. Seconds later, he pulls the rabbit out of the hat.

Now guess how another popular magic trick is done. Making someone "float" in the air seems very hard. Actually, it is one of the easiest tricks to figure out. Can you guess how it is done?

A. Making Decisions

How do you think the trick of making someone seem to float in the air is done? Write a good ending to the story. Explain what you think the magician does. To help explain, add a drawing if you wish.

_____

_____

_____

_____

_____

_____

_____

_____

_____

_____

_____

_____

_____

_____

_____

B. About You

Describe a magic trick or show you have seen in person or on television. If you need help writing your ideas, ask your teacher. Keep your writing in your journal.

Review of Lessons 11–15

Word Study

A. Vowel Sounds

Write the word that fits best in each sentence. Choose from the words below.

chalk	daughter	lawn	sausage
small	south	vows	

1. We cooked _____ instead of bacon to go with our eggs.

2. Fred's _____ is older than his son.

3. I really like to mow the _____ during the summer.

4. Lisa's directions said to turn _____ on Sixth Street.

5. We needed some _____ to write on the board.

6. The couple said their wedding _____ without a mistake.

7. Please get two _____ bananas for breakfast.

B. Multiple Meanings

Look at three different meanings for *present*:

a. to be in a certain place

b. to introduce or give

c. a gift

Write the letter of the meaning that best fits the way *present* is used in each sentence.

_____ 1. Keisha wanted to present her ideas to her boss.

_____ 2. The present was wrapped in purple paper.

_____ 3. Since everyone was present the meeting could begin.

Comprehension

A. Main Idea

Read the paragraph. Underline the sentence that is the main idea.

1. Sugar became very important during World War II. People were asked to do without it. Since most people eat a great deal of the sweet stuff, this was asking a lot. This was not because it was needed to make candy bars for the troops. Sugar was needed in making the gunpowder that fired bullets and shells.

2. It seems that every group of young people uses words that only they understand. Some of the words are made up. Others are old words used in new ways. We call such words *slang*. One writer said that slang is "language that takes off its coat, spits on its hands, and goes to work." Others feel that slang destroys our language.

B. Drawing Conclusions

Decide which conclusions you can draw from the paragraphs about sugar and slang. Fill in the circle beside your answer.

1. You can conclude that during a war

Ⓐ nothing changes for most people.

Ⓑ sugar is the most important thing to have.

Ⓒ people have to do without some things they usually have.

2. You can conclude that slang is a subject that

Ⓐ people generally agree on.

Ⓑ people have different opinions about.

Ⓒ people always understand.

Pronunciation Key

Use the following pronunciation key to help you say the new words in this book. Each word below is divided into syllables by small dots. When you say a word of two or more syllables, stress the syllable shown in capital letters.

Symbol	Example
a	back (bak)
a	Asia (AY•zhuh)
ar	car (kar)
aw	ball (bawl)
k	corn (korn)
ch	china (CHY•nuh)
eh	pet (peht)
ee	marine (muh•REEN)
ehr	bare (behr)
er	pearl (perl)
ih	did (dihd)
ih	system (SIHS•tuhm)
eye	iris (EYE•ris)
ah	rock (rahk)
oh	rainbow (RAYN•boh)
oy	coin (koyn)
ow	fountain (FOWN•tuhn)
s	spice (spys)
sh	motion (MOH•shuhn)
uh	study (STUHD•ee)
u	full (ful)
oo	cute (kyoot)

Glossary

bond page 105 (bahnd) something that ties two things together

border page 69 (BOHR•duhr) the part around the edge

calorie page 53 (KAL•uh•ree) a measure of the energy in food

character page 23 (KAR•ihk•tuhr) someone in a book, movie, or cartoon

criminal page 77 (KRIHM•uh•nuhl) a person who breaks the law

crumple page 45 (KRUM•puhl) to crush together

double page 53 (DUHB•uhl) twice as much

earthquake page 45 (URTH•kwayk) very hard shaking of the earth

gerbil page 7 (JER•buhl) a small animal much like a mouse

gnaw page 83 (naw) to chew

heave page 45 (heev) to lift with great force

humble page 70 (HUM•buhl) not proud

illustration page 69 (ihl•uh•STRAY•shuhn) a drawing or picture

impress page 77 (ihm•PRES) to get someone's attention

initial page 69 (ih•NIHSH•uhl) first letter of a name

kidnap page 39 (KIHD•nap) to hold a person against his or her will

language page 15 (LANG•gwihj) the sounds and movements we use to talk to each other

liquor page 39 (LIHK•uhr) drink that contains alcohol

magician page 111 (muh•JIHSH•uhn) person who does magic tricks

monster page 24 (MAHN•stuhr) a huge, dangerous person or animal

mount page 105 (mownt) a horse someone rides

nervous page 16 (NER•vuhs) not at ease

nightmare page 23 (NEYET•mayr) a scary dream

nosy page 7 (NOH•zee) getting into someone else's business

nursery page 62 (NUR•suh•ree) place where babies are cared for

outlaw page 77 (OWT•law) to make something against the law; a person who does not obey the law

professional page 111 (proh•FEHSH•uh•nuhl) done as a job

realize page 61 (REE•uh•leyez) to understand

relax page 32 (ree•LAKS) to rest or take it easy

shred page 7 (shrehd) tear into tiny pieces

stepdaughter page 91 (STEHP•dawter) the daughter of the person one is married to

stepmother page 91 (STEHP•muhther) a woman married to one's real father

stepparent page 92 (stehp•PAR•uhnt) a person who has married one's real mother or father

strife page 99 (streyef) fighting or arguing

video page 31 (VIHD•ee•oh) pictures made for television

worthless page 7 (WERTH•lihs) not good or valuable

Steps in the Writing Process

Writing is a process. Following these five steps will help you get from an idea to finished writing.

☑ **STEP 1: Prewriting.** This means you'll do some planning before you begin to write.

• **Choose a topic and purpose.** What will you write about? Why are you writing? You might write to tell a story, to give information, to describe someone, or to persuade someone to do something.

• **Choose your audience.** Who is going to read your writing? You'll write to a friend in a different tone than you'll write to your boss at work.

• **Decide what to say about your topic.** There are several ways to get ideas for what to say . One way is to brainstorm. Ask yourself questions about what you could write about. Write down all the ideas that come to you. Other ways are talking to other people to get their ideas, reading or watching videotapes about your topic, or making a list or outline of things you want to write about.

☑ **STEP 2: Writing the first draft.** Get your ideas down on paper in sentences and paragraphs. Don't worry about spelling and punctuation yet. Write a good topic sentence for each paragraph. A topic sentence tells the main idea of the paragraph. Add facts, examples, or reasons as details to support the topic sentence.

☑ **STEP 3: Editing and revising.** Carefully read what you've written. Does it make sense? Have you used complete sentences? Can you rewrite anything to make your meaning clearer? Can you add anything? Can you take anything out that doesn't really belong?

☑ **STEP 4: Writing the final draft.** First, check for errors. Are spelling and punctuation correct? Then make a final copy.

☑ **STEP 5: Sharing.** The final step in the writing process is sharing your work with others. This is often called *publishing* the piece. You might read your work to others or have them read it.

Answer Key

Lesson 1 • Pages 6–13

Page 6
Predictions will vary.

Page 9
A.
1. face	2. place	3. elephant
4. gerbil	5. cellar	6. cereal
7. phone	8. ginger	9. center
10. gym		

Page 10
B.
1. pick	2. pretty	3. want
4. order	5. drop	6. final
7. nap	8. correct	9. enjoy
10. tear	11. stays	

Page 11
1. A
2. Answers will vary but details may include:
   Tom has worked at the shelter for three years.
   He feeds the animals and cleans their cages.
   He helps people find pets.
   He really likes animals.
   He is good at his job.

Page 12
1. F	2. O	3. O	4. F
5. F	6. O	7. O	8. F

Page 13
B. Writing you do in your journal is just for you. There are no right or wrong answers. You need not show your journal writing to anyone unless you wish; discuss this with your teacher.

Lesson 2 • Pages 14–21

Page 14
Predictions will vary.

Page 16
Penny and Fred, page 15; Jane and Scott, page 14; Eddie and Rose, page 16.

Page 17
A.
1. hobby	2. apply	3. lady
4. shy	5. fancy	6. happy
7. sorry	8. probably	9. plenty
10. really	11. easy	12. ready

Page 18
B.
1. many	2. cross	3. true
4. stand	5. Most	6. front
7. nervous	8. louder	9. long
10. common		

Page 19
A.
1. B	2. C	3. C	4. B

Page 20
B. 1. Fact 1: We may cross our arms or legs while talking to someone we do not like.
Fact 2: We may rub our noses when we think someone is not telling the truth.
Fact 3: We stand over someone as we talk to tell them "I am the boss."
Fact 4: Looking into someone's eyes as we talk tells them we speak the truth.
2. C

Page 21
A. Andy was very good at reading body language. Andy paid special attention to people's eyes and hands as they talked. He could pick out someone who would talk to him by watching the person from across the room. ~~Andy also liked to watch baseball games.~~ He knew how to tell if a person was telling the truth.
Paragraphs will vary.

B. Writing you do in your journal is just for you. There are no right or wrong answers. You need not show your journal writing to anyone unless you wish; discuss this with your teacher.

Lesson 3 • Pages 22–29

Page 22

Predictions will vary.

Page 25

A. 1. awake 2. carrots 3. organ
   4. sailor 5. shovel 6. spiders
   7. pilot 8. circus 9. tigers
   10. happen

Page 26

B. 1. darkness 2. fright 3. harmed
   4. accept 5. trouble

C. 1. The sound of a child's scream can wake a parent faster than anything else.
   2. It is up to the parent to decide which TV shows are OK to watch.
   3. A child may believe anything a parent says.

Page 27

A. 1. When children see a dog on a show who is run over by a truck, they think the dog is really hurt. They think a car crash on TV is real, and they may have bad dreams about it. If they see a show about a child who loses his mother, they worry about the child and ask if he finds his mother. Very young children confuse television with real life.

   2. By doing just three things, parents can help their child sleep better. They can be careful that the child doesn't watch TV shows that could be upsetting. Parents can be careful about what they say to the child, too. They can also talk to the child about anything the child fears. They can explain that many scary things are only make-believe.

B. 1. O 2. F 3. O 4. F
   5. O 6. F

Page 28

C. 1. A 2. C

Page 29

A. Paragraphs will vary.

B. Writing you do in your journal is just for you. There are no right or wrong answers. You need not show your journal writing to anyone unless you wish; discuss this with your teacher.

Lesson 4 • Pages 30–37

Page 30

Predictions will vary.

Page 33

A. 1. write 2. wrists 3. wrong
   4. know 5. knuckle 6. wrestle
   7. knock 8. knee 9. wrap
   10. wreck

Page 34

B. 1. auto 2. motor 3. clocks
   4. shops 5. cost 6. work

C. 1. Computers are everywhere you look today.
   2. The use of computers will grow as time goes on.
   3. Computers need a small space to store a lot of facts.
   4. After a long, hard day on the job, most people want to go home and rest.

Page 35

A. 1. C 2. A 3. B
B. B

Page 36

C. 1. C 2. A 3. B
D. 1. O 2. F 3. O 4. O
   5. F 6. F

Page 37

A. Ideas will vary.

B. Writing you do in your journal is just for you. There are no right or wrong answers. You need not show your journal writing to anyone unless you wish; discuss this with your teacher.

Lesson 5 • Pages 38–41

Page 38
Predictions will vary.

Page 41

A. Ideas will vary.

B. Writing you do in your journal is just for you. There are no right or wrong answers. You need not show your journal writing to anyone unless you wish; discuss this with your teacher.

Review 1–5 • Pages 42–43

Page 42
A. 1. lemon   2. cactus   3. engine
   4. camera   5. shovel
B. 1. dirt   2. boxes   3. wash
   4. shakes
C. 1. smooth   2. speedy   3. hot
   4. right

Page 43
A. 3
B. 1. F   2. O   3. F   4. O
   5. F

Lesson 6 • Pages 44–51

Page 44
Predictions will vary.

Page 47
A. 1. world   2. hurt   3. farms
   4. work   5. curb   6. worry

7. firm   8. anger   9. stir
10. answer

Page 48

B. An earthquake strikes so (quickly) it catches people by surprise. That is one reason people are so (deeply) afraid of earthquakes. One minute people are sleeping (quietly). The next their world is crashing (loudly) around them. There are things that can help people live (safely) through earthquakes. For one thing, homes must be (strongly) built. Also, people should know (exactly) what to do in an earthquake. Even then, they may (barely) escape with their lives.

C. 1. fully   2. clearly   3. surely
   4. likely   5. slowly

Page 49
A. 2 Something snapped deep in the earth.
   1 Diane Stillman was asleep.
   3 Diane's dresser pinned her to the bed.
B. 1. C   2. C

Page 50
C. 1. B   2. A

Page 51
A. Many people think that earthquakes happen only in California, but this is not true. Earthquakes can happen anywhere. ~~Many storms happen in the Pacific Ocean.~~ One of the largest earthquakes in North America struck along the Mississippi River. Small earthquakes strike many places in the United States, Canada, and Mexico every year.

B. Writing you do in your journal is just for you. There are no right or wrong answers. You need not show your journal writing to anyone unless you wish; discuss this with your teacher.

Lesson 7 • Pages 52–59

Page 52
Predictions will vary.

Page 55
A. 1. health   2. eager   3. appear
4. ahead   5. easy   6. ready
7. increase   8. clear   9. peace
10. team   11. meals

Page 56
B. 1. disregard   2. disappear
3. discomfort   4. disagree
5. dissatisfied   6. dislike
7. dishonest   8. disobey

Page 57
A. 1. what will happen if Victor keeps eating this way.
2. what health problems are caused by eating too much fast food.
B. 1. Victor ordered a double bacon cheeseburger with special sauce, fries, super size soda, and a fried apple pie.
2. Victor wanted to eat right away.
3. Victor will let his belt out a notch because he ate too much.

Page 58
C. 1. A   2. B   3. C
D. 1. C   2. B

Page 59
A. Paragraphs will vary but should contain supporting details such as eating at places that offer low-calorie meals, eating foods with less fat, and avoiding fried foods.
B. Writing you do in your journal is just for you. There are no right or wrong answers. You need not show your journal writing to anyone unless you wish; discuss this with your teacher.

Lesson 8 • Pages 60–67

Page 60
Predictions will vary.

Page 63
A. 1. holiday   2. rescue   3. highway
4. pie   5. value   6. due
7. play   8. die   9. glue
10. blues   11. tried

Page 64
B. It is needless to feel that weekends are endless. Regardless of who you are, you can find ways to fill up the time. You can give some of your time at a shelter for the homeless. Helping others keeps you from feeling worthless, because you know you are doing good. If you are having sleepless nights because you are friendless, do something! Change a joyless time into a happy time.
1. restless   2. lawless   3. harmless
4. jobless   5. hopeless   6. countless
7. thoughtless

Page 65
A. 1. C   2. C   3. B
B. 1. B   2. A

Page 66
C. 1. C, D
2. Beto whistled and sang wherever he went. He always had a cheerful "Hello!" for everyone. Whenever there was a hard job to be done, Beto was there to help. On weekends he ran errands for people who could not get out. Beto was never too busy to help someone.
3. A, D

Page 67
A. Paragraphs will vary.
B. Writing you do in your journal is just for you. There are no right or wrong answers.

You need not show your journal writing to anyone unless you wish; discuss this with your teacher.

Lesson 9 • Pages 68–75

Page 68
Predictions will vary.

Page 71
A. 1. care   2. career   3. search
4. steer   5. hair   6. wear
7. pair   8. fair   9. learn
10. earn

Page 72
B.   Have you ever gotten a greeting card when you were feeling (gloomy)? Perhaps it just came on a (rainy) day. Knowing someone was thinking of you can make your eyes all (teary.) Cards do not have to be (wordy.) Some are (corny,) or some are (funny.) But all of them help to make an (achy) heart feel better.
1. funny   2. silly   3. noisy
4. handy   5. leafy   6. flowery
7. sticky   8. scary

Page 73
A. 2, 3, 5
B. 1. Mary likes to draw in the afternoons.
2. The people who make and sell goods with her drawings on them get most of the money.
3. Mary makes phone calls in the mornings.
4. Mary spends evenings with her husband and two sons.

Page 74
C. 3 Mary started her own business.
2 Mary got a job at a store that sold art supplies.
1 Mary started drawing.
4 Mary's husband quit his job to help her.
1. A   2. C
D. 1. F   2. O   3. F   4. O

Page 75
A. Paragraphs will vary.
B.   Writing you do in your journal is just for you. There are no right or wrong answers. You need not show your journal writing to anyone unless you wish; discuss this with your teacher.

Lesson 10 • Pages 76–79

Page 76
Predictions will vary.

Page 79
A. Answers will vary.
B.   Writing you do in your journal is just for you. There are no right or wrong answers. You need not show your journal writing to anyone unless you wish; discuss this with your teacher.

Review 6–10 • Pages 80–81

Page 80
A. 1. earth   2. year   3. twirl
4. perch   5. shirt   6. porch
7. firm   8. chart
B. 1. fearless   2. soundly   3. spicy
4. winless   5. handy   6. extremely

Page 81
A. 2 Sybil had a holiday.
3 Sybil went to work early.
1 Sybil got to work late.
B. 1. We were tired, (so we went to bed early.)
2. (I was late to work) because my alarm clock did not go off.
3. Since there are five Fridays next month, (I will get five paychecks.)
4. The hot sun (made us very thirsty.)
5. (The freeway bridge fell down) when the earthquake shook the ground.

6. Thunder made the dog hide under the bed.

7. The ceiling fell in after the water pipe in the attic burst.

8. We moved to this city because I got a job here.

9. The sound of the door creaking sent chills up my spine.

10. Since the elevator was overloaded, the door would not close.

Lesson 11 • Pages 82–89

Page 82
Predictions will vary.

Page 85
A. 1. fault   2. caught   3. stall
   4. awkward   5. also   6. talk
   7. cause   8. small   9. dawn
   10. awful   11. walk

Page 86
B. 1. d   2. b   3. c   4. a
C. 1. b   2. a   3. c

Page 87
A. 1. B   2. B   3. C
B. 1.   It is usually better to forgive someone who has hurt you. As long as you stay angry, you are hurting yourself. Also, your anger becomes a second problem. So then you have two problems, being hurt and being angry.

2.   Kate was angry. She had been hurt, and she could not get over it. She was also upset with herself for feeling this way. She couldn't sleep or do her work. Kate had to forgive Hal to make things right again.

Page 88
C. 1. B   2. C
D. Fact 1: Kate said the whole thing was Hal's fault.
Fact 2: Kate said if Hal had told her the truth, she would have been angry, but that would have passed.
Fact 3: Kate said when Hal lied to her, it destroyed her trust in him, and she blamed him for that.
Circle conclusion number 2, Things would have been better if Hal had not lied.

Page 89
A. Paragraphs will vary but should include these four details: talk every day, share worries, tell the truth, and respect yourself and each other.
B.   Writing you do in your journal is just for you. There are no right or wrong answers. You need not show your journal writing to anyone unless you wish; discuss this with your teacher.

Lesson 12 • Pages 90–97

Page 90
Predictions will vary.

Page 93
A. 1. fights   2. thought   3. right
   4. though   5. weight   6. brought
   7. might   8. neighbor   9. through
   10. delight   11. sigh

Page 94
B. 1. A   2. B   3. B   4. A
   5. B   6. A   7. B   8. B

Page 95
A. 1. B   2. A   3. B
B. 1.   A child shouldn't be made to call a new stepparent "Mom" or "Dad." The child still needs to love his or her real parent. One way to handle this is to

suggest the child call the stepparent by his or her first name. Some children like to use a name like "Daddy Jim."

2. Some people try to prove to the children that they are part of a "real" family by giving the same last name to all the children. Some children don't like this, since it seems to say their birth parent isn't important. Children should decide for themselves when they are 16 or older.

Page 96
C. I. D   2. D
D. I. A   2. B

Page 97
A. Ideas and paragraphs will vary.
B. Writing you do in your journal is just for you. There are no right or wrong answers. You need not show your journal writing to anyone unless you wish; discuss this with your teacher.

Lesson 13 • Pages 98–103

Page 98
Predictions will vary.

Page 100
I. look   2. fall   3. troubled
4. far away

Page 101
A. I. B   2. A
B. I. B   2. B   3. B

Page 102
C. I. C   2. B

Page 103
A. Answers will vary.

B. Writing you do in your journal is just for you. There are no right or wrong answers. You need not show your journal writing to anyone unless you wish; discuss this with your teacher.

Lesson 14 • Pages 104–109

Page 104
Predictions will vary.

Page 106
A. I. found   2. Now   3. blouse
4. outfits   5. couch   6. flowers
7. doubt   8. sound   9. However
10. cowboy   II. brown

Page 107
A. I. B   2. C
B. I. O   2. F   3. O   4. F

Page 108
C. I. Circle *rock, cloud, mount, bond*.
2. Circle *road, river, tree, treasure*.
3. Circle *gift, prize, safe place, guest*.
D. I. Circle *car, magic carpet*.
2. Circle *words, knives*.
3. Circle *snake, question mark*.
4. Circle *joy, balloon*.

Page 109
A. Answers will vary.
B. Writing you do in your journal is just for you. There are no right or wrong answers. You need not show your journal writing to anyone unless you wish; discuss this with your teacher.

Lesson 15 • Pages 110–113

Page 110
Predictions will vary.

Page 113

A.   Answers will vary. The person is held up by a hidden bar. Usually a hoop is passed around the person to prove nothing is holding her up. The trick is knowing how to turn the hoop so that it only seems as though it passed all the way around her body.

B.   Writing you do in your journal is just for you. There are no right or wrong answers. You need not show your journal writing to anyone unless you wish; discuss this with your teacher.

Review 11–15 • Pages 114–115

Page 114

A. I. sausage   2. daughter   3. lawn
     4. south   5. chalk   6. vows
     7. small

B. I. b   2. c   3. a

Page 115

A. I.   Sugar became very important during World War II. People were asked to do without it. Since most people eat a great deal of the sweet stuff, this was asking a lot. This was not because it was needed to make candy bars for the troops. Sugar was needed in making the gunpowder that fired bullets and shells.

     2.   It seems that every group of young people uses words that only they understand. Some of the words are made up. Others are old words used in new ways. We call such words *slang*. One writer said that slang is "language that takes off its coat, spits on its hands, and goes to work." Others feel that slang destroys our language.

B. I. C   2. B

Lesson	Page	Reading Skill		Number Correct
1	9	**Word Study:**	A. Consonant Sounds	_____ out of 10
	10		B. Synonyms	_____ out of 11
	11	**Comprehension:**	A. Main Idea	_____ out of 2
	12		B. Facts and Opinions	_____ out of 8
2	17	**Word Study:**	A. Vowel Sounds	_____ out of 12
	18		B. Antonyms	_____ out of 10
	19	**Comprehension:**	A. Passage Details	_____ out of 4
	20		B. Drawing Conclusions	_____ out of 2
3	25	**Word Study:**	A. Vowel Sounds	_____ out of 10
	26		B. Synonyms	_____ out of 5
	26		C. Antonyms	_____ out of 3
	27	**Comprehension:**	A. Main Idea	_____ out of 2
	27		B. Facts and Opinions	_____ out of 6
	28		C. Author's Purpose	_____ out of 2
4	33	**Word Study:**	A. Consonant Sounds	_____ out of 10
	34		B. Synonyms	_____ out of 6
	34		C. Antonyms	_____ out of 4
	35	**Comprehension:**	A. Passage Details	_____ out of 3
	35		B. Author's Purpose	_____ out of 1
	36		C. Drawing Conclusions	_____ out of 3
	36		D. Facts and Opinions	out of 6
Review	42	**Word Study:**	A. Vowel Sounds	_____ out of 5
	42		B. Synonyms	_____ out of 4
	42		C. Antonyms	_____ out of 4
	43	**Comprehension:**	A. Main Idea	_____ out of 1
	43		B. Facts and Opinions	_____ out of 5
6	47	**Word Study:**	A. Vowel Sounds	_____ out of 10
	48		B–C. Suffixes	_____ out of 13
	49	**Comprehension:**	A–B. Sequence	_____ out of 4
	50		C. Cause and Effect	_____ out of 2
7	55	**Word Study:**	A. Vowel Sounds	_____ out of 11
	56		B. Prefixes	_____ out of 8
	57	**Comprehension:**	A. Author's Purpose	_____ out of 2
	57		B. Passage Details	_____ out of 3
	58		C. Cause and Effect	_____ out of 3
	58		D. Drawing Conclusions	_____ out of 2

Lesson	Page	Reading Skill		Number Correct
8	63	**Word Study:**	A. Vowel Sounds	_____ out of 11
	64		B. Suffixes	_____ out of 15
	65	**Comprehension:**	A. Sequence	_____ out of 3
	65		B. Drawing Conclusions	_____ out of 2
	66		C. Character Traits	_____ out of 3
9	71	**Word Study:**	A. Vowel Sounds	_____ out of 10
	72		B. Suffixes	_____ out of 15
	73	**Comprehension:**	A. Character Traits	_____ out of 1
	73		B. Passage Details	_____ out of 4
	74		C. Sequence	_____ out of 3
	74		D. Facts and Opinions	_____ out of 4
Review	80	**Word Study:**	A. Vowel Sounds	_____ out of 8
	80		B. Suffixes	_____ out of 6
	81	**Comprehension:**	A. Sequence	_____ out of 1
	81		B. Cause and Effect	_____ out of 10
11	85	**Word Study:**	A. Vowel Sounds	_____ out of 11
	86		B–C. Multiple Meanings	_____ out of 7
	87	**Comprehension:**	A. Passage Details	_____ out of 3
	87		B. Main Idea	_____ out of 2
	88		C. Author's Purpose	_____ out of 3
	88		D. Drawing Conclusions	_____ out of 2
12	93	**Word Study:**	A. Consonant Sounds	_____ out of 11
	94		B. Multiple Meanings	_____ out of 8
	95	**Comprehension:**	A. Passage Details	_____ out of 3
	95		B. Main Idea	_____ out of 2
	96		C. Author's Purpose	_____ out of 2
	96		D. Drawing Conclusions	_____ out of 2
13	100	**Word Study:**	Words in Context	_____ out of 4
	101	**Comprehension:**	A. Character Traits	_____ out of 2
	101		B. Drawing Conclusions	_____ out of 3
	102		C. Metaphors	_____ out of 2
14	106	**Word Study:**	Vowel Sounds	_____ out of 11
	107	**Comprehension:**	A. Drawing Conclusions	_____ out of 2
	107		B. Facts and Opinions	_____ out of 4
	108		C–D. Metaphors	_____ out of 7
Review	114	**Word Study:**	A. Vowel Sounds	_____ out of 7
	114		B. Multiple Meanings	_____ out of 3
	115	**Comprehension:**	A. Main Idea	_____ out of 2
	115		B. Drawing Conclusions	_____ out of 2